Interactive Notebooks

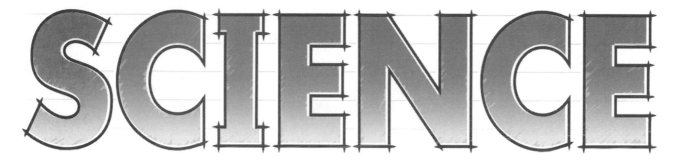

SCIENCE

Grade 2

Credits

Author: Natalie Rompella
Content Editors: Elise Craver, Chris Schwab, Angela Triplett

Visit *carsondellosa.com* for correlations to Common Core, state, national, and Canadian provincial standards.

Carson-Dellosa Publishing LLC
PO Box 35665
Greensboro, NC 27425 USA
carsondellosa.com

978-1-4838-3122-0
05-216207784

Table of Contents

What Are Interactive Notebooks?

Interactive notebooks are a unique form of note taking. Teachers guide students through creating pages of notes on new topics. Instead of being in the traditional linear, handwritten format, notes are colorful and spread across the pages. Notes also often include drawings, diagrams, and 3-D elements to make the material understandable and relevant. Students are encouraged to complete their notebook pages in ways that make sense to them. With this personalization, no two pages are exactly the same.

Because of their creative nature, interactive notebooks allow students to be active participants in their own learning. Teachers can easily differentiate pages to address the levels and needs of each learner. The notebooks are arranged sequentially, and students can create tables of contents as they create pages, making it simple for students to use their notebooks for reference throughout the year. The interactive, easily personalized format makes interactive notebooks ideal for engaging students in learning new concepts.

Using interactive notebooks can take as much or as little time as you like. Students will initially take longer to create pages but will get faster as they become familiar with the process of creating pages. You may choose to only create a notebook page as a class at the beginning of each unit, or you may choose to create a new page for each topic within a unit. You can decide what works best for your students and schedule.

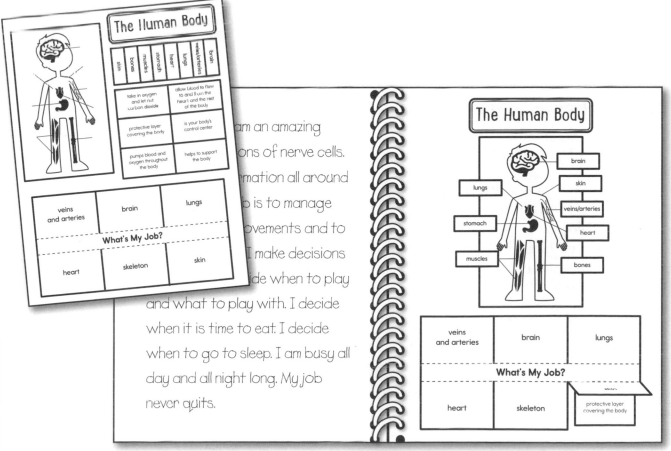

A student's interactive notebook for the human body

Getting Started

You can start using interactive notebooks at any point in the school year. Use the following guidelines to help you get started in your classroom. (For more specific details, management ideas, and tips, see page 10.)

1. **Plan each notebook.**

   Use the planning template (page 9) to lay out a general plan for the topics you plan to cover in each notebook for the year.

2. **Choose a notebook type.**

   Interactive notebooks are usually either single-subject, spiral-bound notebooks, composition books, or three-ring binders with loose-leaf paper. Each type presents pros and cons. See page 5 for a more in-depth look at each type of notebook.

3. **Allow students to personalize their notebooks.**

   Have students decorate their notebook covers, as well as add their names and subjects. This provides a sense of ownership and emphasizes the personalized nature of the notebooks.

4. **Number the pages and create the table of contents.**

   Have students number the bottom outside corner of each page, front and back. When completing a new page, adding a table of contents entry will be easy. Have students title the first page of each notebook "Table of Contents." Have them leave several blank pages at the front of each notebook for the table of contents. Refer to your general plan for an idea of about how many entries students will be creating.

5. **Start creating pages.**

   Always begin a new page by adding an entry to the table of contents. Create the first notebook pages along with students to model proper format and expectations.

This book contains individual topics for you to introduce. Use the pages in the order that best fits your curriculum. You may also choose to alter the content presented to better match your school's curriculum. The provided lesson plans often do not instruct students to add color. Students should make their own choices about personalizing the content in ways that make sense to them. Encourage students to highlight and color the pages as they desire while creating them.

After introducing topics, you may choose to add more practice pages. Use the reproducibles (pages 78–96) to easily create new notebook pages for practice or to introduce topics not addressed in this book.

Use the grading rubric (page 11) to grade students' interactive notebooks at various points throughout the year. Provide students copies of the rubric to glue into their notebooks and refer to as they create pages.

What Type of Notebook Should I Use?

Spiral Notebook

The pages in this book are formatted for a standard one-subject notebook.

Pros

- Notebook can be folded in half.
- Page size is larger.
- It is inexpensive.
- It often comes with pockets for storing materials.

Cons

- Pages can easily fall out.
- Spirals can snag or become misshapen.
- Page count and size vary widely.
- It is not as durable as a binder.

Tips

- Encase the spiral in duct tape to make it more durable.
- Keep the notebooks in a central place to prevent them from getting damaged in desks.

Composition Notebook

Pros

- Pages don't easily fall out.
- Page size and page count are standard.
- It is inexpensive.

Cons

- Notebook cannot be folded in half.
- Page size is smaller.
- It is not as durable as a binder.

Tips

- Copy pages meant for standard-sized notebooks at 85 or 90 percent. Test to see which works better for your notebook.

Binder with Loose-Leaf Paper

Pros

- Pages can be easily added, moved, or removed.
- Pages can be removed individually for grading.
- You can add full-page printed handouts.
- It has durable covers.

Cons

- Pages can easily fall out.
- Pages aren't durable.
- It is more expensive than a notebook.
- Students can easily misplace or lose pages.
- Larger size makes it more difficult to store.

Tips

- Provide hole reinforcers for damaged pages.

How to Organize an Interactive Notebook

You may organize an interactive notebook in many different ways. You may choose to organize it by unit and work sequentially through the book. Or, you may choose to create different sections that you will revisit and add to throughout the year. Choose the format that works best for your students and subject.

An interactive notebook includes different types of pages in addition to the pages students create. Non-content pages you may want to add include the following:

Title Page

This page is useful for quickly identifying notebooks. It is especially helpful in classrooms that use multiple interactive notebooks for different subjects. Have students write the subject (such as "Science") on the title page of each interactive notebook. They should also include their full names. You may choose to have them include other information such as the teacher's name, classroom number, or class period.

Table of Contents

The table of contents is an integral part of the interactive notebook. It makes referencing previously created pages quick and easy for students. Make sure that students leave several pages at the beginning of each notebook for a table of contents.

Expectations and Grading Rubric

It is helpful for each student to have a copy of the expectations for creating interactive notebook pages. You may choose to include a list of expectations for parents and students to sign, as well as a grading rubric (page 11).

Unit Title Pages

Consider using a single page at the beginning of each section to separate it. Title the page with the unit name. Add a tab (page 78) to the edge of the page to make it easy to flip to the unit. Add a table of contents for only the pages in that unit.

Glossary

Reserve a six-page section at the back of the notebook where students can create a glossary. Draw a line to split in half the front and back of each page, creating 24 sections. Combine Q and R and Y and Z to fit the entire alphabet. Have students add an entry as each new vocabulary word is introduced.

Formatting Student Notebook Pages

The other major consideration for planning an interactive notebook is how to treat the left and right sides of a notebook spread. Interactive journals are usually viewed with the notebook open flat. This creates a left side and a right side. You have several options for how to treat the two sides of the spread.

Traditionally, the right side is used for the teacher-directed part of the lesson, and the left side is used for students to interact with the lesson content. The lessons in this book use this format. However, you may prefer to switch the order for your class so that the teacher-directed learning is on the left and the student input is on the right.

It can also be important to include standards, learning objectives, or essential questions in interactive notebooks. You may choose to write these on the top-left side of each page before completing the teacher-directed page on the right side. You may also choose to have students include the "Introduction" part of each lesson in that same top-left section. This is the *in, through, out* method. Students enter *in* the lesson on the top left of the page, go *through* the lesson on the right page, and exit *out* of the lesson on the bottom left with a reflection activity.

The following chart details different types of items and activities that you could include on each side.

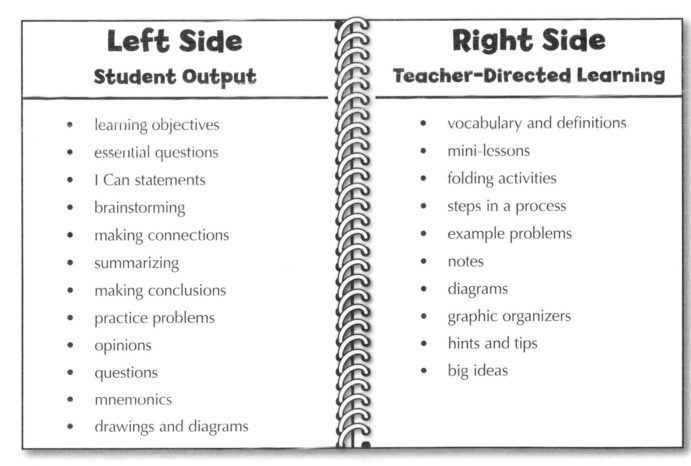

Left Side **Student Output**	**Right Side** **Teacher-Directed Learning**
• learning objectives	• vocabulary and definitions
• essential questions	• mini-lessons
• I Can statements	• folding activities
• brainstorming	• steps in a process
• making connections	• example problems
• summarizing	• notes
• making conclusions	• diagrams
• practice problems	• graphic organizers
• opinions	• hints and tips
• questions	• big ideas
• mnemonics	
• drawings and diagrams	

Planning for the Year

Making a general plan for interactive notebooks will help with planning, grading, and testing throughout the year. You do not need to plan every single page, but knowing what topics you will cover and in what order can be helpful in many ways.

Use the Interactive Notebook Plan (page 9) to plan your units and topics and where they should be placed in the notebooks. Remember to include enough pages at the beginning for the non-content pages, such as the title page, table of contents, and grading rubric. You may also want to leave a page at the beginning of each unit to place a mini table of contents for just that section.

In addition, when planning new pages, it can be helpful to sketch the pieces you will need to create. Use the following notebook template and notes to plan new pages.

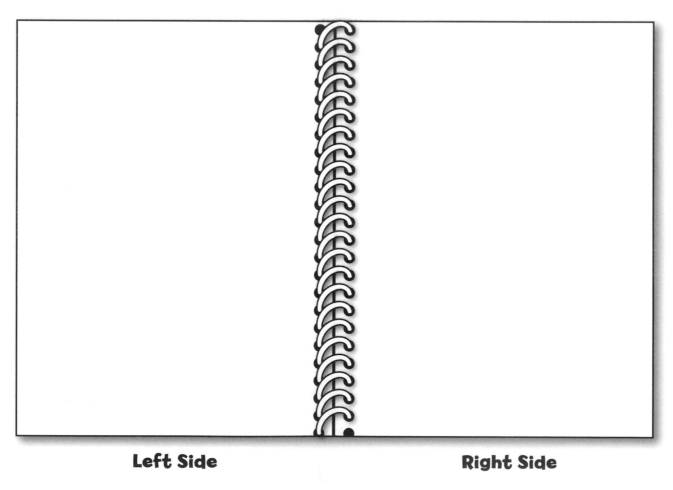

Left Side   **Right Side**

Notes

_____

_____

_____

Interactive Notebook Plan

Page	Topic	Page	Topic
1		51	
2		52	
3		53	
4		54	
5		55	
6		56	
7		57	
8		58	
9		59	
10		60	
11		61	
12		62	
13		63	
14		64	
15		65	
16		66	
17		67	
18		68	
19		69	
20		70	
21		71	
22		72	
23		73	
24		74	
25		75	
26		76	
27		77	
28		78	
29		79	
30		80	
31		81	
32		82	
33		83	
34		84	
35		85	
36		86	
37		87	
38		88	
39		89	
40		90	
41		91	
42		92	
43		93	
44		94	
45		95	
46		96	
47		97	
48		98	
49		99	
50		100	

Managing Interactive Notebooks in the Classroom

Working with Younger Students

- Use your yearly plan to preprogram a table of contents that you can copy and give to students to glue into their notebooks, instead of writing individual entries.

- Have assistants or parent volunteers precut pieces.

- Create glue sponges to make gluing easier. Place large sponges in plastic containers with white glue. The sponges will absorb the glue. Students can wipe the backs of pieces across the sponges to apply the glue with less mess.

Creating Notebook Pages

- For storing loose pieces, add a pocket to the inside back cover. Use the envelope pattern (page 81), an envelope, a jumbo library pocket, or a resealable plastic bag. Or, tape the bottom and side edges of the two last pages of the notebook together to create a large pocket.

- When writing under flaps, have students trace the outline of each flap so that they can visualize the writing boundary.

- Where the dashed line will be hidden on the inside of the fold, have students first fold the piece in the opposite direction so that they can see the dashed line. Then, students should fold the piece back the other way along the same fold line to create the fold in the correct direction.

- To avoid losing pieces, have students keep all of their scraps on their desks until they have finished each page.

- To contain paper scraps and avoid multiple trips to the trash can, provide small groups with small buckets or tubs.

- For students who run out of room, keep full and half sheets available. Students can glue these to the bottom of the pages and fold them up when not in use.

Dealing with Absences

- Create a model notebook for absent students to reference when they return to school.

- Have students cut a second set of pieces as they work on their own pages.

Using the Notebook

- To organize sections of the notebook, provide each student with a sheet of tabs (page 78).

- To easily find the next blank page, either cut off the top-right corner of each page as it is used or attach a long piece of yarn or ribbon to the back cover to be used as a bookmark.

Interactive Notebook Grading Rubric

4
- _____ Table of contents is complete.
- _____ All notebook pages are included.
- _____ All notebook pages are complete.
- _____ Notebook pages are neat and organized.
- _____ Information is correct.
- _____ Pages show personalization, evidence of learning, and original ideas.

3
- _____ Table of contents is mostly complete.
- _____ One notebook page is missing.
- _____ Notebook pages are mostly complete.
- _____ Notebook pages are mostly neat and organized.
- _____ Information is mostly correct.
- _____ Pages show some personalization, evidence of learning, and original ideas.

2
- _____ Table of contents is missing a few entries.
- _____ A few notebook pages are missing.
- _____ A few notebook pages are incomplete.
- _____ Notebook pages are somewhat messy and unorganized.
- _____ Information has several errors.
- _____ Pages show little personalization, evidence of learning, or original ideas.

1
- _____ Table of contents is incomplete.
- _____ Many notebook pages are missing.
- _____ Many notebook pages are incomplete.
- _____ Notebook pages are too messy and unorganized to use.
- _____ Information is incorrect.
- _____ Pages show no personalization, evidence of learning, or original ideas.

Living and Nonliving

Living and Nonliving

Introduction

Ask students for examples of things that are living. Then, ask what makes something alive. Discuss the characteristics of living things, such as living things breathe, grow, are made of cells, reproduce, and respond and adapt to their environments. Ask for examples of living and nonliving things.

Creating the Notebook Page

Guide students through the following steps to complete the right-hand page in their notebooks.

1. Add a Table of Contents entry for the Living and Nonliving pages.

2. Cut out the title and glue it to the top of the page.

3. Cut out the *Living things* accordion fold. Starting with the *Living things* section on top, accordion fold on the dashed lines. Apply glue to the back of the last section and attach it to the right side of the page below the title.

4. Cut out the flap books. For each flap book, cut on the solid lines to create three flaps. Apply glue to the back of each left section. Attach them to the page so that the spine of each one is slightly underneath the other, creating two nine-flap books.

5. Under each flap, write whether the object is living (L) or nonliving (N). It may be helpful to discuss plants such as mushrooms and carrots, which are living while planted but nonliving in a grocery store setting where many students may be familiar with them. If an object was once living but is no longer alive, write *nonliving (N)*. Write three more objects on the blank flaps. Then, write the answers under the flaps.

Reflect on Learning

To complete the left-hand page, have students answer the following question: *How do plants and animals use nonliving things?*

Answer Key
Nonliving: car, lightning, log, paper, rock, TV, water, wind; Living: baby, bee, carrot, mushroom, puppy, tree, seaweed

© Carson-Dellosa • CD-104906

Living and Nonliving

Living things

are made of cells,

breathe,

grow and reproduce,

respond and adapt to their environment.

Living or Nonliving?

TV	log	lightning
wind	tree	carrot
puppy	mushroom	baby

Living or Nonliving?

car	bee	
rock	paper	
water	seaweed	

Plant and Animal Needs

Ask students what they need to survive. Have them write their answers on self-stick notes. Draw a T-chart on the board with the headings *Wants* and *Needs*. Have students come to the board and put their responses below the correct category. Finally, discuss and compare plant and animal needs with human needs.

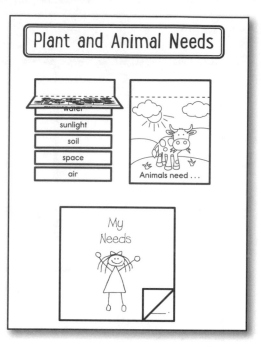

Creating the Notebook Page

Guide students through the following steps to complete the right-hand page in their notebooks.

1. Add a Table of Contents entry for the Plant and Animal Needs pages.

2. Cut out the title and glue it to the top of the page.

3. Cut out the *Plants need . . .* and *Animals need . . .* flaps. Apply glue to the back of each top section and attach them below the title.

4. Cut out the 14 word cards. Read each need. Then, glue it under the correct flap. Extra pieces may be discarded.

5. Cut out the *I drink* piece. Fold the left side over the text on the dashed line. Apply glue to the back of the piece and attach it to the bottom of the page.

6. On the front, write *My Needs* and draw a picture of yourself. On the inside of the book, fill in the blanks with your needs.

Reflect on Learning

To complete the left-hand page, have students pretend they are hiking overnight. Have them create a list of what they would pack. Have them circle which of those items are needed to survive.

Answer Key
Plants Needs: air, soil, space, sunlight, water; Animals Needs: air, food, shelter, space, water

Plant and Animal Needs

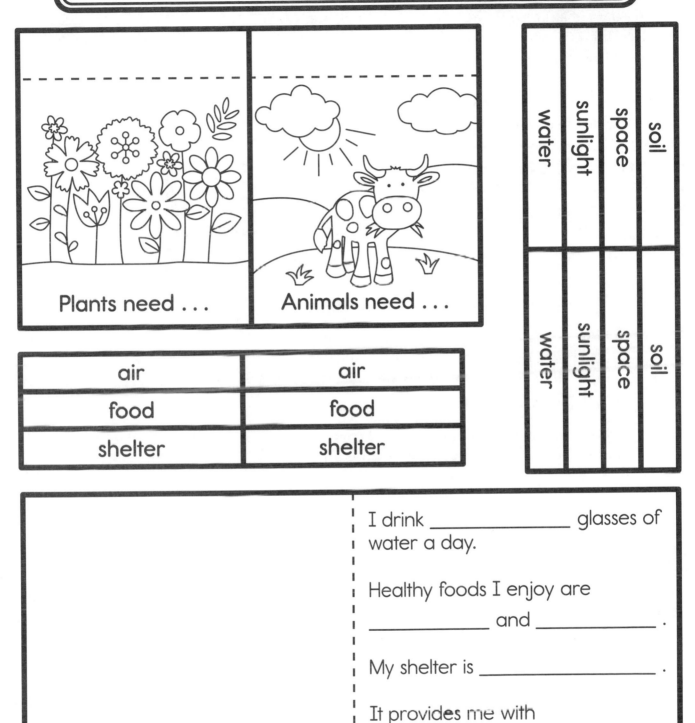

air	air
food	food
shelter	shelter

Plants need . . .

Animals need . . .

water	sunlight	space	soil

water	sunlight	space	soil

I drink _____ glasses of water a day.

Healthy foods I enjoy are _____ and _____ .

My shelter is _____ .

It provides me with

_____ .

I breathe in _____ .

Parts of a Plant

Introduction

Draw a diagram of a simple flower and label its parts on the board (roots, stem, flower, leaf). Discuss what each part of a plant does to keep the plant alive. Then, play a game of "four corners" to assess students' understanding. Assign each corner of the room a part of a plant. Read the definition of each part of a plant and have students move to the correct corner of the room.

Creating the Notebook Page

Guide students through the following steps to complete the right-hand page in their notebooks.

1. Add a Table of Contents entry for the Parts of a Plant pages.

2. Cut out the title and glue it to the top of the page.

3. Cut out the parts-of-a-plant flaps. Assemble them in the correct order. Apply glue to the back of the tabs and attach them on the left side of the page, creating a flower.

4. Under each flap, write the name of the plant part.

5. Cut out the flap book. Cut on the solid lines to create four flaps. Fold the flaps on the dashed lines so that the flaps cover the definitions. Apply glue to the back of the right side and attach it on the right side of the page.

6. Read each definition. Write the correct plant part on the front of each flap.

Reflect on Learning

To complete the left-hand page, provide each student with several pictures of plants. Have students look at the pictures and discuss with partners what is the same about the plants (they have leaves, they have a stem, etc.) and what is different (they have different colored petals, the number of leaves, etc.). Then, have each student choose one picture to cut out and glue into his notebook. He should label the picture of the plant with the correct parts.

Parts of a Plant

	gives plants support; moves water and nutrients to other plant parts
	petals help to attract pollinators, who help create fruit and seeds
	absorb water from the soil and draw it up to the rest of the plant
	takes in carbon dioxide and gives off oxygen; makes food for plants

Animal Structures

Introduction

Discuss the different structures of animals, such as feet, fins, wings, backbones, etc. Distribute pictures of various animals from magazines or printed from the Internet to each student. Pair students together. Have them complete Venn diagrams comparing the structures of their two animals.

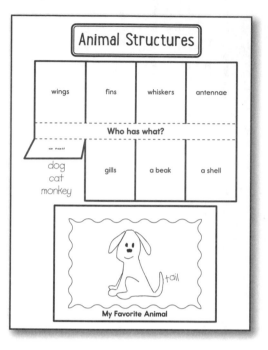

Creating the Notebook Page

Guide students through the following steps to complete the right-hand page in their notebooks.

1. Add a Table of Contents entry for the Animal Structures pages.

2. Cut out the title and glue it to the top of the page.

3. Cut out the *Who has what?* flap book. Cut on the solid lines to create eight flaps. Apply glue to the back of the middle section and attach it below the title.

4. Under each flap, write the name of at least one animal with that particular structure.

5. Cut out the *My Favorite Animal* picture frame. Glue it to the bottom of the page.

6. Draw a picture of your favorite animal. Label its structures.

Reflect on Learning

To complete the left-hand page, have students write a list of parts on plants and animals that are similar. Have them choose one and write a sentence to tell what purpose it serves for each.

18

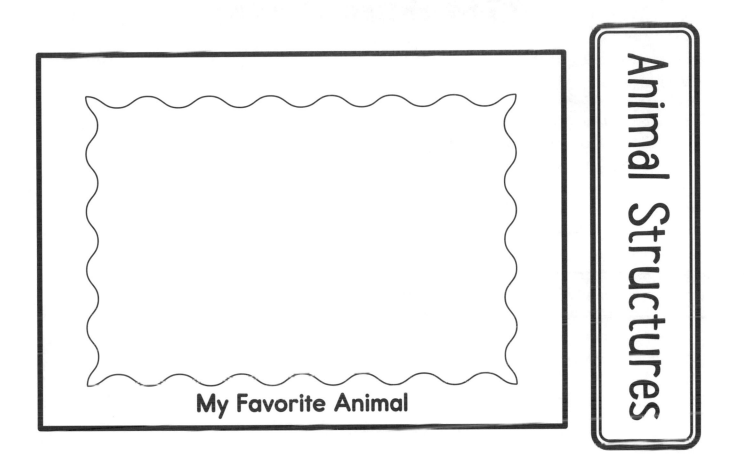

My Favorite Animal

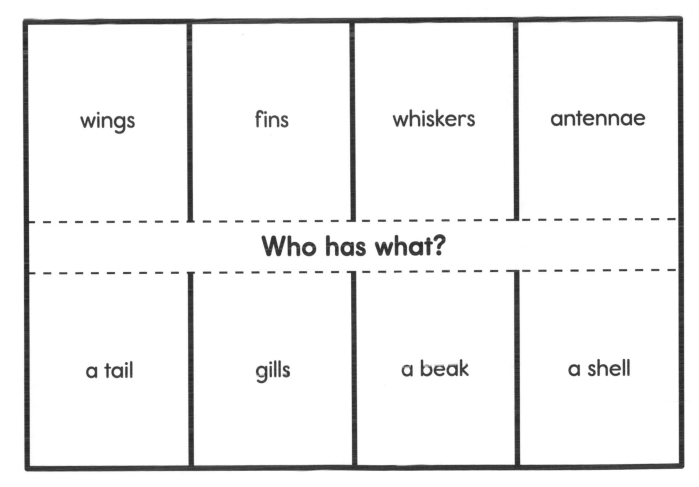

wings	fins	whiskers	antennae

Who has what?

a tail	gills	a beak	a shell

The Human Body

Introduction

Have students run in place for 30 seconds. Ask them if they can feel their hearts beating faster. Explain that the heart helps to pump blood through the body. Have students run again. Ask if they notice they are breathing air in and out. Explain that oxygen is being drawn into their lungs, and unneeded carbon dioxide is being blown out. Discuss how the body has many structures that help it to function.

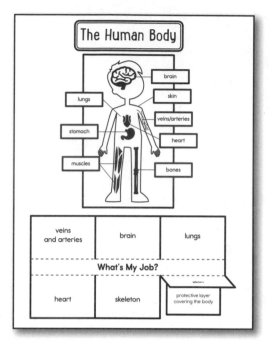

Creating the Notebook Page

Guide students through the following steps to complete the right-hand page in their notebooks.

1. Add a Table of Contents entry for The Human Body pages.

2. Cut out the title and glue it to the top of the page.

3. Cut out the human body piece and glue it below the title.

4. Cut out the eight body parts labels. Glue the labels to the correct place on the human body piece.

5. Cut out the *What's My Job?* flap book. Cut on the solid lines to create six flaps. Apply glue to the back of the middle section and attach it to the bottom of the page.

6. Cut out the six definition pieces. Find the correct definition for each body part and glue it under the correct flap.

Reflect on Learning

To complete the left-hand page, have students choose a body part from the right-hand page and write a job description from that organ's point of view. Students should describe who they are and what jobs they do in the body.

Answer Key
veins and arteries: allow blood to flow to and from the heart and the rest of the body; brain: is your body's control center; lungs: take in oxygen and let out carbon dioxide; heart: pumps blood and oxygen throughout the body; skeleton: helps to support the body; skin: protective layer covering the body

The Human Body

skin	bones	muscles	stomach	heart	lungs	veins/arteries	brain

take in oxygen and let out carbon dioxide	allow blood to flow to and from the heart and the rest of the body
protective layer covering the body	is your body's control center
pumps blood and oxygen throughout the body	helps to support the body

veins and arteries	brain	lungs
What's My Job?		
heart	skeleton	skin

Animal Life Cycles

Introduction

Discuss what the word *cycle* means. Explain that animals have a life cycle. Ask students if they think all animals follow the same life cycle. Review the life cycles of butterflies, chickens, and frogs. Then, have a volunteer act out a mystery animal's life cycle while the rest of the class tries to guess which animal's life cycle is being represented.

Creating the Notebook Page

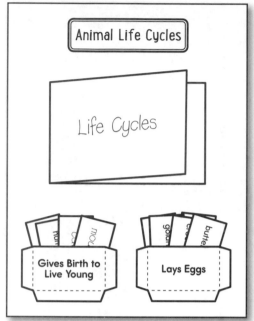

Guide students through the following steps to complete the right-hand page in their notebooks.

1. Add a Table of Contents entry for the Animal Life Cycles pages.

2. Cut out the title and glue it to the top of the page.

3. Cut out the *Dog/Human* piece. Fold in on the dashed line to create a book. Apply glue to the back of the book and attach it below the title.

4. Write *Life Cycles* on the front of the book. On the inside, read the stages of a dog's life cycle. Then, write or draw to show the life cycle of a human. Discuss how dogs and humans look throughout the stages of their life cycles.

5. Cut out the *Birth to Live Young* and *Lays Eggs* pockets. Apply glue to the back of the tabs and attach them near the bottom of the page.

6. Cut out the animal pieces and the two blank pieces. Write the name of another animal on each of the two blank pieces.

7. Sort each animal into the correct pocket.

Reflect on Learning

To complete the left-hand page, have students draw two large overlapping circles to create a Venn diagram. Have them choose two animals and compare and contrast their life cycles.

Answer Key
Birth to Live Young: human, dog; Lays Eggs: butterfly, goldfish, frog, chicken, crocodile

Animal Life Cycles

Gives Birth to Live Young

Lays Eggs

Dog

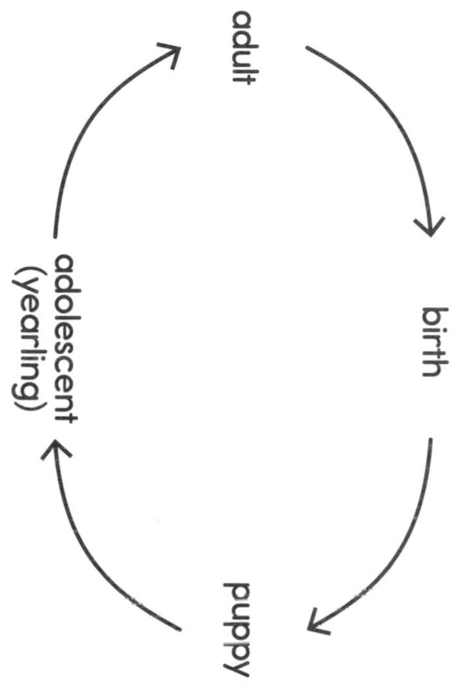

birth

adult

adolescent
(yearling)

puppy

Human

human	dog	chicken
butterfly	frog	goldfish
crocodile		

The Life Cycle of a Butterfly

Introduction

Discuss the life cycle of a butterfly and the term *metamorphosis*. Divide the class into four groups. Assign each group a different stage of the butterfly's life cycle. Have them act out that stage. Arrange the students in a circle on the floor. Have the egg group act out their stage. When they finish, have them sit down and allow the caterpillar group to act out their part. Continue the activity until all of the groups have acted out each stage in turn.

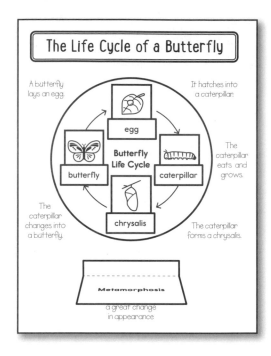

Creating the Notebook Page

Guide students through the following steps to complete the right-hand page in their notebooks.

1. Add a Table of Contents entry for The Life Cycle of a Butterfly pages.

2. Cut out the title and glue it to the top of the page.

3. Cut out the *Butterfly Life Cycle* circle and glue it to the middle of the page below the title.

4. Cut out the four butterfly life cycle picture pieces. Glue them onto the circle in the correct order.

5. Cut out the four word pieces. Glue them under the correct stage of the butterfly life cycle pictures to label each stage.

6. Write information about each stage around the outside of the circle, such as telling at which stage the butterfly eats, lays eggs, changes, and hatches.

7. Cut out the *Metamorphosis* flap. Apply glue to the back of the top section and attach it to the bottom of the page.

8. Under the flap, write the definition of *metamorphosis* (a great change in appearance).

Reflect on Learning

To complete the left-hand page, have students write a story about a butterfly going through its life cycle, beginning when it hatches from an egg and ending when it becomes a butterfly. Allow time for students to share their work.

The Life Cycle of a Butterfly

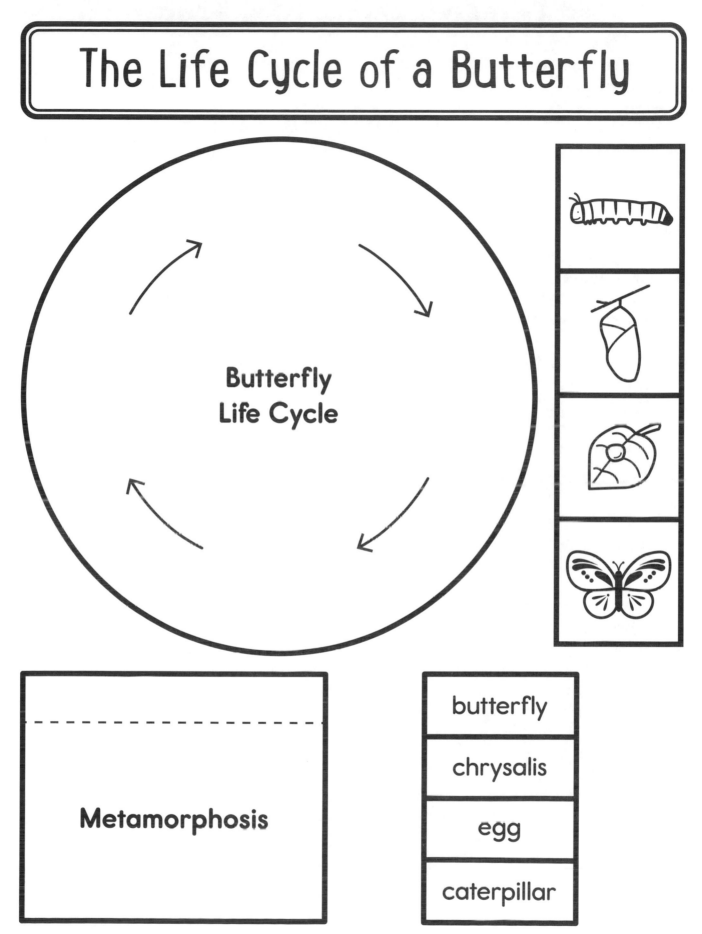

Butterfly Life Cycle

Metamorphosis

butterfly

chrysalis

egg

caterpillar

The Life Cycle of a Frog

Introduction

Discuss the different stages of a frog's life cycle. Draw and label a picture of each stage on four sheets of blank construction paper. Then, have four volunteers come to the front of the room. Give each volunteer one of the four stages. Ask the volunteers to arrange themselves in the correct order. Discuss how the volunteers knew how to stand in the correct order.

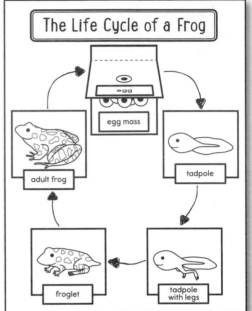

Creating the Notebook Page

Guide students through the following steps to complete the right-hand page in their notebooks.

1. Add a Table of Contents entry for The Life Cycle of a Frog pages.

2. Cut out the title and glue it to the top of the page.

3. Cut out the remaining pieces. (For the egg and egg mass pictures, apply glue to the gray glue area of the egg mass picture and place the single egg picture on top of it.)

4. Glue the words onto the correct pictures.

5. Arrange the pictures in the correct order of a frog's life cycle and glue them to the page.

6. Draw arrows on the page showing the direction of the cycle.

Reflect on Learning

To complete the left-hand page, have students draw two large overlapping circles to create a Venn diagram. Have them draw or write to compare and contrast two stages of the frog's life cycle.

Answer Key
From top: egg mass; egg; tadpole; froglet; young frog; adult frog

tadpole	adult frog
egg mass	tadpole with legs
egg	froglet

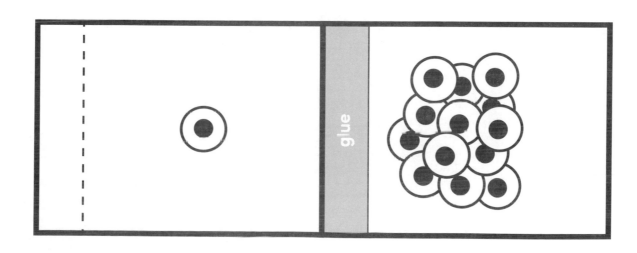

glue

Plant Life Cycles

Introduction

Discuss how, like animals, plants also have a life cycle. If possible, take students on a stages-in-the-life-of-a-tree scavenger hunt. Look for a seedling, a sapling, a young adult tree, and a very mature tree. Have students draw and record what they see on the scavenger hunt on a sheet of paper and label each stage.

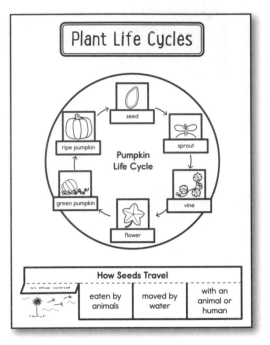

Creating the Notebook Page

Guide students through the following steps to complete the right-hand page in their notebooks.

1. Add a Table of Contents entry for the Plant Life Cycles pages.

2. Cut out the title and glue it to the top of the page.

3. Cut out the *Pumpkin Life Cycle* circle and glue it below the title.

4. Cut out the six pumpkin life cycle picture pieces. Glue them onto the circle in the correct order.

5. Cut out the six word pieces. Glue them under the correct stage of the pumpkin life cycle pictures to label each stage.

6. Cut out the *How Seeds Travel* flap book. Cut on the solid lines to create four flaps. Apply glue to the back of the top section and attach it to the bottom of the page.

7. Under each flap, draw a picture of how a seed travels in this way.

Reflect on Learning

To complete the left-hand page, have students compare and contrast the life cycle of a plant to an animal of their choosing. Allow time for students to share their work.

28

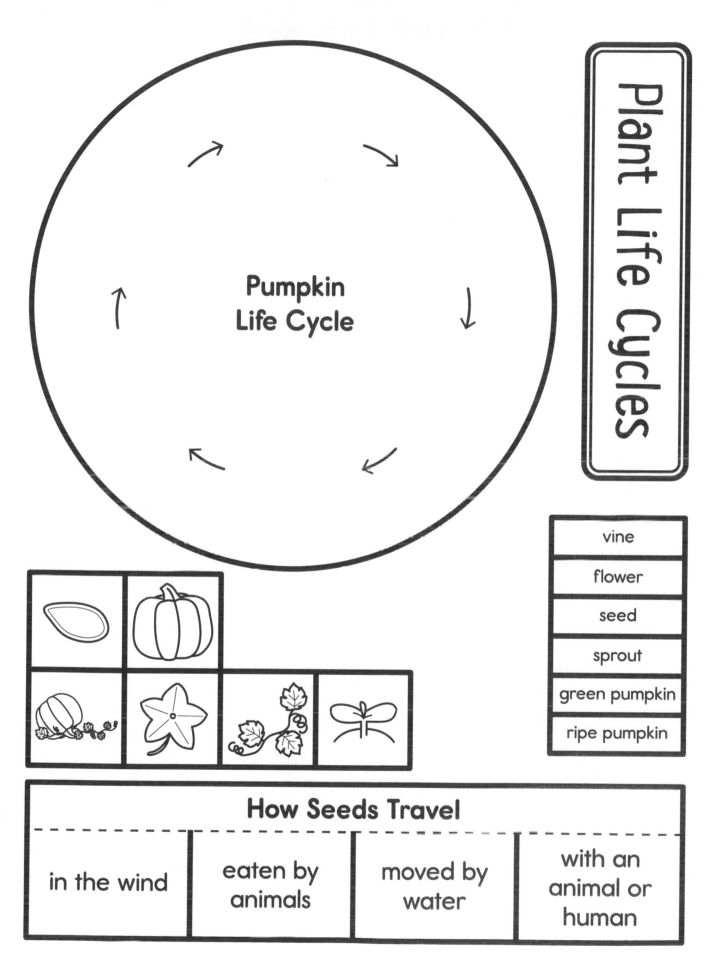

Pumpkin
Life Cycle

vine
flower
seed
sprout
green pumpkin
ripe pumpkin

How Seeds Travel

in the wind	eaten by animals	moved by water	with an animal or human

Plants We Eat

Introduction

Review the parts of plants (roots, stem, leaves, flowers, seeds, fruit). Ask students to share what they ate for breakfast. Write the answers on the board. Have students come up to the board and circle one food or dish that came from a plant.

Creating the Notebook Page

Guide students through the following steps to complete the right-hand page in their notebooks.

1. Add a Table of Contents entry for the Plants We Eat pages.

2. Cut out the title and glue it to the top of the page.

3. Cut out the *Roots/Stems* fold-up book. Fold the two sides in to the center on the dashed lines. Apply glue to the back of the *Stems/Leaves/Fruits* section and attach it below the title.

4. Cut out the fruits and vegetables pieces. Think about what part of the plant each food is and glue it into the book below the correct heading.

5. Write one more additional food under each heading.

6. Cut out the *What Plants Are You Eating?* flap book. Cut on the solid lines to create three flaps. Apply glue to the back of the top section and attach it to the bottom of the page.

7. Draw a picture of each of the three foods on the front of each flap above the word.

8. Under each flap, write the ingredients in the food that comes from plants. Add at least one fruit or vegetable to the food to make it healthier. For example, add broccoli to pizza.

Reflect on Learning

To complete the left-hand page, have students brainstorm or invent a dish that includes three different plant parts. Have them write a recipe for it. Tell what plant parts are used.

Answer Key
roots: carrot, potato; stems: asparagus, celery; leaves: lettuce, spinach; seeds: corn, peas; fruits: apple, pumpkin

Plants We Eat

carrot	celery
lettuce	apple
corn	potato
asparagus	spinach
pumpkin	peas

What Plants Are You Eating?

pizza	taco	banana bread

Roots	**Stems**	**Leaves**	**Fruits**	**Seeds**

Habitats

Introduction

Distribute index cards with the names of animals on them to the students. Discuss with students what a habitat is and what it provides for an animal. Have students brainstorm the habitats of their animals. Then, have students move around and find other students whose animals share similar habitats to their animals.

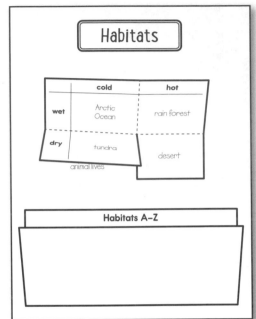

Creating the Notebook Page

Guide students through the following steps to complete the right-hand page in their notebooks.

1. Add a Table of Contents entry for the Habitats pages.

2. Cut out the title and glue it to the top of the page.

3. To the bottom left of the title, define a habitat (the place where a plant or animal lives).

4. Cut out the *cold/hot* piece. Cut on the solid line. Apply glue to the back of the bottom right section and attach it below the title to the right of the definition.

5. Fill in each box with a place that fits the description (wet/cold, wet/hot, dry/cold, and dry/hot). Fold down the top two sections. Then, fold the left side in. Write *Extreme Habitats* on the top section.

6. Cut out the *Habitats A–Z* piece. Fold up on the dashed line. Apply glue to the back of the top section and attach it below the *Extreme Habitats* piece.

7. Write a different habitat for each letter of the alphabet. The habitats can be very specific (oak leaf) or general (rain forest).

Reflect on Learning

To complete the left-hand page, write the following sentences on the board: *My favorite animal is a _____ . It lives _____ . It needs this habitat because _____* . Then, have students copy the sentences and fill in the blanks to complete them. Finally, students should draw pictures of their animals in their environments.

Habitats

	cold	hot
wet		
dry		

Habitats A-Z

A _____   N _____
B _____   O _____
C _____   P _____
D _____   Q _____
E _____   R _____
F _____   S _____
G _____   T _____
H _____   U _____
I _____   V _____
J _____   W _____
K _____   X _____
L _____   Y _____
M _____   Z _____

Adaptations

Each student will need a sharpened pencil and a paper clip to complete the spinner activity.

Introduction

Explain the definition of *adaptation* as the process of changing something to become better suited to its environment. Ask students what they could do to adapt to waiting outside for the bus to arrive on a rainy day. Possible answers may include carrying an umbrella or wearing a raincoat. Discuss how animals do not have a coat to put on when it is raining. Have students brainstorm what animals and plants might have instead to protect themselves and help them adapt to their environments.

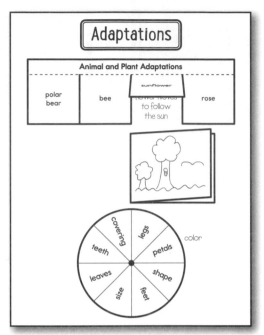

Creating the Notebook Page

Guide students through the following steps to complete the right-hand page in their notebooks.

1. Add a Table of Contents entry for the Adaptations pages.

2. Cut out the title and glue it to the top of the page.

3. Cut out the flap book. Cut on the solid lines to create four flaps. Apply glue to the back of the top section and attach it below the title.

4. Under each flap, describe an adaptation each animal or plant has, considering its various structures and the environment in which it lives.

5. Cut out the *Animal/Adaptation* piece. Fold in on the dashed line to create a book. Apply glue to the back of the book and attach it below the flap book.

6. On the front, draw a picture of a natural area you have seen before. On the inside below the word *Animal*, write the names of two animals that could live in that area. Next to each animal's name, write an adaptation on the *Adaptation* side that helps it to survive.

7. Cut out the circle spinner and glue it to the bottom half of the page.

8. Use a sharpened pencil and a paper clip to spin the spinner. Whatever plant or animal structure the spinner lands on, think of how it is unique to a specific plant or animal. For example, if the spinner lands on *teeth* you may write *beavers have sharp teeth to chew wood.* Write the answers on the page around the spinner.

Reflect on Learning

To complete the left-hand page, have students write about two adaptations human bodies have and how they are helpful to us.

Adaptations

Animal and Plant Adaptations

polar bear	bee	sunflower	rose

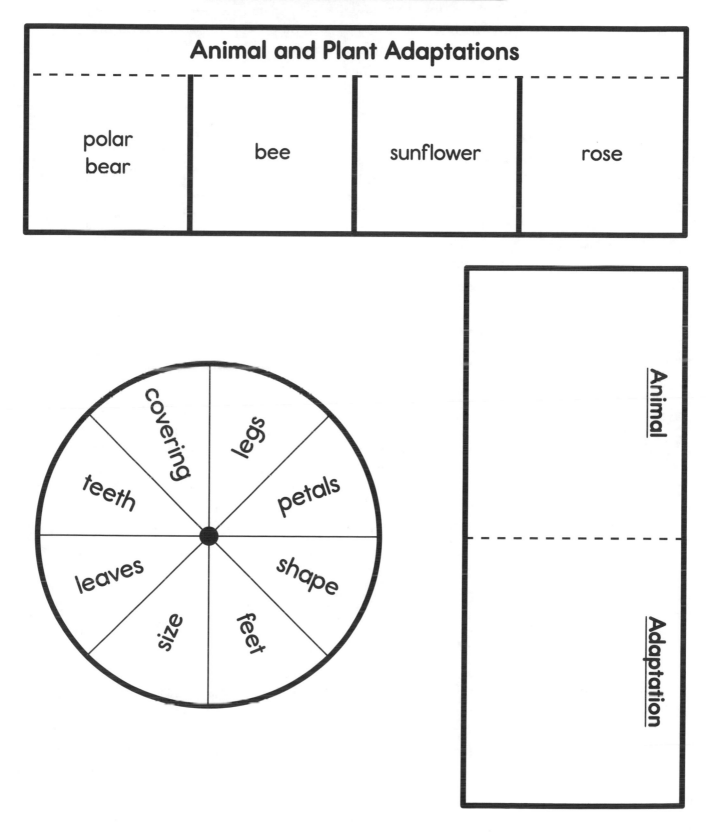

Animal

Adaptation

Interdependence

Introduction

Ask students for examples of ways we use plants and animals. Discuss how plants, animals, and humans interact with each other and need one another for survival. Write the names of various plants and animals on index cards. Create three concentric circles with yarn. Label the three circles *Plants*, *Animals*, and *Humans*. Have volunteers come to the front of the class one at a time and choose an index card. Next, have the volunteers throw a beanbag into the circles. Whichever one it lands in, they must tell a way in which their plant or animal interacts with a plant, animal, or human.

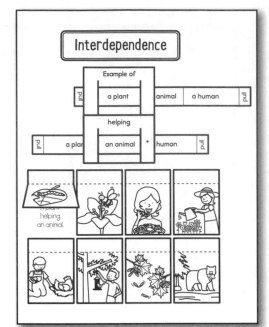

Creating the Notebook Page

Guide students through the following steps to complete the right-hand page in their notebooks.

1. Add a Table of Contents entry for the Interdependence pages.

2. Cut out the title and glue it to the top of the page.

3. Cut out the two *a plant/an animal/a human* strips. Cut out the *Example of* piece. Cut on the solid lines to create three flaps. Slide a *a plant/an animal/a human* strip over the center flap so that one word shows at a time in the center of the blank side. Without removing the strip, apply glue to the top and bottom of the back of the piece. (Do not apply glue to the space covered by the _____ strip or it will not slide freely.) Attach it to the top of the page. Repeat the steps with the *helping* piece and the remaining strip. Attach it directly below the other strip so the two form a sentence: *Example of [a plant] helping [an animal]*.

4. Cut out the flaps. Apply glue to the back of the top sections of each flap. Attach them in two rows at the bottom of the page.

5. Using the two sliders, slide the strips to create an interdependent relationship. Find a picture that matches that relationship. Under each flap, write the type of interdependence: *A _____ helping a _____* . There are nine possible combinations. The only relationship not shown is a human helping a human.

Reflect on Learning

To complete the left-hand page, have students answer the following question: *Why is it important for humans to protect plants and animals?* Then, have students write a sentence about a time they took care of a plant or animal.

Interdependence

Example of

helping

pull	pull
a plant	a plant
an animal	an animal
a human	a human
pull	pull

Traits

Introduction

Explain the definition of a trait as a quality, feature, or other thing that distinguishes a person, animal, or plant. Traits can include hair color, eye color, beak shape, tooth shape, etc. Explain that physical traits are passed down from generation to generation and are called inherited traits. Acquired traits, like learning to speak another language, are traits that have to be learned or obtained. Draw two circles on the board labeled *Inherited* and *Acquired*. Provide several volunteers with self-stick notes programmed with inherited and acquired traits such as *green eyes*, *brown hair*, *fast runner*, *stripes*, etc. Have volunteers come to the board and place their self-stick notes in the appropriate circles.

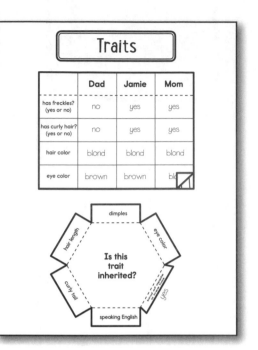

Creating the Notebook Page

Guide students through the following steps to complete the right-hand page in their notebooks.

1. Add a Table of Contents entry for the Traits pages.

2. Cut out the title and glue it to the top of the page.

3. Cut out the *Dad/Jamie/Mom* chart. Apply glue to the back of the top section and attach it below the title. Cut out the picture and glue it under the flap.

4. Looking at the picture, fill in the chart with the inherited traits of Jamie's family. Discuss which trait Jamie inherited from each parent.

5. Cut out the *Is this trait inherited?* flap book. Apply glue to the back of the middle section and attach it to the bottom of the page.

6. Under each flap, write *yes* or *no* to tell if the trait is inherited or not.

Reflect on Learning

To complete the left-hand page, have students create a T-chart labeled *Behaviors Humans Learn* and *Traits Humans Inherit*. Have students work in pairs to fill in the T-charts. Allow time for students to share their work.

dimples

hair length

eye color

Is this
trait
inherited?

curly tail

kind of apple
a tree has

speaking English

Traits

	Dad	Jamie	Mom
has freckles? (yes or no)			
has curly hair? (yes or no)			
hair color			
eye color			

Jamie's dad

brown eyes

blond hair

Jamie

brown eyes

blond hair

Jamie's mom

blue eyes

blond hair

Good Health

Introduction

Have students brainstorm ways to be healthy. Record their ideas on the board. Then, work together as a class to categorize the ideas into related groups, such as food choices, types of exercise, etc.

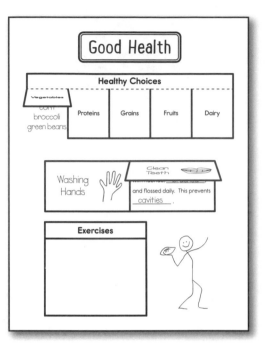

Creating the Notebook Page

Guide students through the following steps to complete the right-hand page in their notebooks.

1. Add a Table of Contents entry for the Good Health pages.

2. Cut out the title and glue it to the top of the page.

3. Cut out the *Healthy Choices* flap book. Cut on the solid lines to create five flaps. Apply glue to the back of the top section and attach it below the title.

4. Under each flap, write examples of healthy foods that fit the category.

5. Cut out the *Hands should be* flap book. Cut on the solid line to create two flaps. Fold two flaps down on the dashed lines to cover the text. Apply glue to the back of the bottom half and attach it below the *Healthy Choices* flap book.

6. Fill in the blanks with the missing words. (Possible answers may include: Hands should be washed with soap and water before **dinner** and after **playing**. Teeth should be **brushed** with fluoride **toothpaste** and flossed daily. This prevents **cavities**.) On the left flap, draw a picture of a hand and write the words *Washing Hands*. On the right flap, draw a picture of teeth and write the words *Clean Teeth*.

7. Cut out the *Exercises* piece. Apply glue to the back of the top section and attach it to the bottom-left side of the page.

8. Write the name of an exercise or a way to get your heart pumping on each line. Put a check next to the ones you enjoy doing. Fold up the bottom half of the piece. To the right, draw a picture of yourself exercising.

Reflect on Learning

To complete the left-hand page, have each student create a poster showing ways to be healthy related to diet, exercise, keeping clean, and having healthy teeth. Allow time for students to share their work.

Good Health

Exercises

- ☐ _____
- ☐ _____
- ☐ _____
- ☐ _____
- ☐ _____

- ☐ _____
- ☐ _____
- ☐ _____
- ☐ _____

Teeth should be _____ with fluoride, _____, and flossed daily. This prevents _____.

Hands should be washed with _____ and water before _____ and after _____.

Healthy Choices

Vegetables	Proteins	Grains	Fruits	Dairy

Matter

Introduction

Hold up an object, such as a pencil or a shoe. Have students describe it. Have each student try to say something different about the object. Discuss how objects can be described and compared in many ways. Inflate a balloon or blow into a clear plastic bag. Ask students to describe what's inside. Explain that both the pencil and the air are types of matter. Matter is anything that takes up space and has mass.

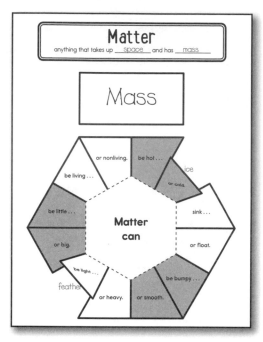

Creating the Notebook Page

Guide students through the following steps to complete the right-hand page in their notebooks.

1. Add a Table of Contents entry for the Matter pages.

2. Cut out the title and glue it to the top of the page.

3. Complete the definition of matter (anything that takes up **space** and has **mass**).

4. Cut out the rectangular flap book. Fold the left side on the dashed line to cover the definition. Apply glue to the back and attach it below the title. On the front, write the word *Mass*.

5. Cut out the *Matter can* piece. Cut on the solid lines to create twelve flaps. Apply glue to the back of the middle section and attach it to the bottom of the page.

6. Under each flap, write an example of a type of matter that fits the description.

Reflect on Learning

To complete the left-hand page, provide students with magazines or newspapers. Have each student cut out two pictures of examples of matter. Then, students should glue the pictures in their notebooks and compare and contrast the two examples of matter by describing their properties.

Matter

anything that takes up _____ and has _____

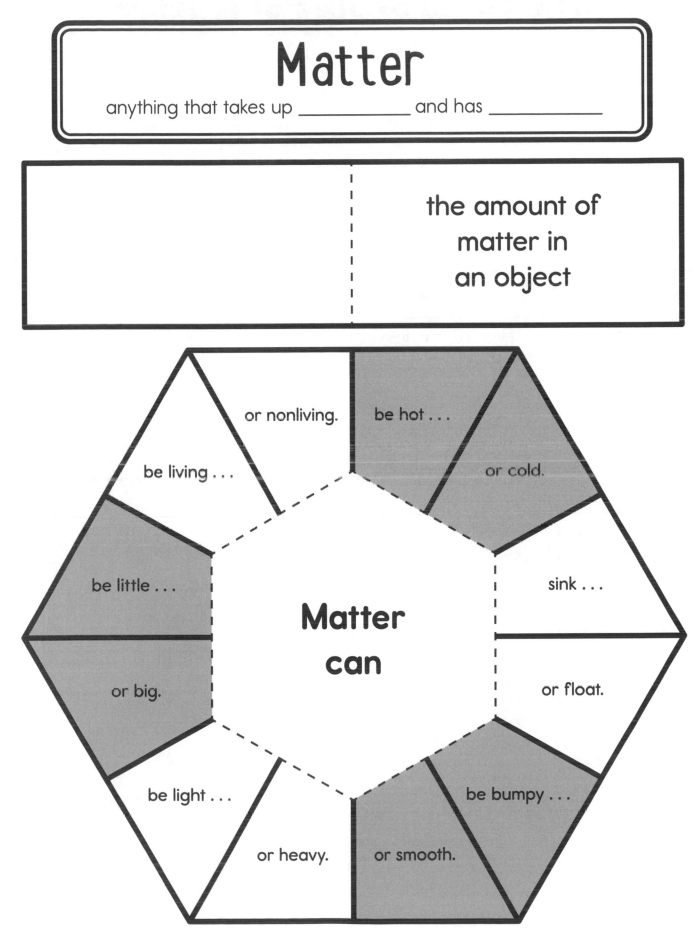

the amount of
matter in
an object

or nonliving.

be hot . . .

or cold.

be living . . .

be little . . .

sink . . .

Matter
can

or big.

or float.

be light . . .

be bumpy . . .

or heavy.

or smooth.

The Three States of Matter

Review the three states of matter with students: solid, liquid, and gas. Distribute self-stick notes to each student. Have students look around the room and use the self-stick notes to label objects as solids, liquids, or gases. When complete, discuss which there was the most of: solids, liquids, or gases. Remind students that the air we breathe is a gas. Discuss examples of other gases, such as helium inside a balloon and car exhaust.

Creating the Notebook Page

Guide students through the following steps to complete the right-hand page in their notebooks.

1. Add a Table of Contents entry for The Three States of Matter pages.

2. Cut out the title and glue it to the top of the page.

3. Cut out the *Solid/Liquid/Gas* flap book. Cut on the solid lines to create three flaps. Apply glue to the back of the top section and attach it to the page below the title.

4. Under each flap, draw an example of the state of matter.

5. Cut out the flap book with the pictures. Cut on the solid lines to create three flaps. Fold on the dashed line so that the flaps cover the answer spaces. Apply glue to the back of the left section and attach it to the bottom of the page.

6. Write the answer for each definition under the flap.

Reflect on Learning

To complete the left-hand page, have students create three riddles that describe a mystery solid, a mystery liquid, and a mystery gas. Have them put their answers upside down on the bottom of the page. Then, have students switch notebooks with a partner and solve the riddles.

Answer Key
From top to bottom: gas; solid; liquid

The Three States of Matter

Solid	Liquid	Gas

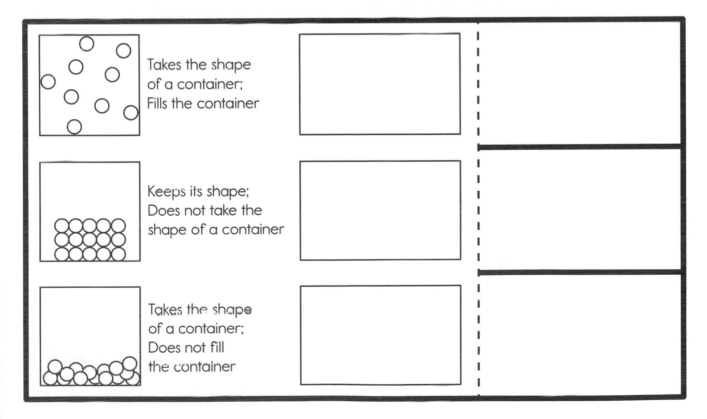

Takes the shape of a container; Fills the container

Keeps its shape; Does not take the shape of a container

Takes the shape of a container; Does not fill the container

Changing States of Matter

Display a glass of ice and let it sit untouched through the introduction. Review the three states of matter. Ask what type of matter chocolate is. Ask students what would happen if it were left out in the sun. Explain that this is an example of matter changing forms. Ask what type of matter orange juice is. Ask what would happen if it were placed in the freezer overnight. Question what would happen if a small pan of water was left in the sun on a hot day. Last, ask what would happen if a glass of ice water sat in a warm room. Show the ice and discuss what happened to it during the discussion. Explain that these are all examples of how matter can change states.

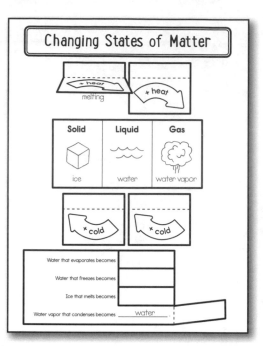

Creating the Notebook Page

Guide students through the following steps to complete the right-hand page in their notebooks.

1. Add a Table of Contents entry for the Changing States of Matter pages.

2. Cut out the title and glue it to the top of the page.

3. Cut out the *Solid Liquid Gas* piece. Glue it below the title, leaving enough space to glue two of the *+ heat* flaps above it.

4. Draw and label water as a solid, liquid, and gas in each of the blank squares.

5. Cut out the *+ heat* and *+ cold* flaps. Apply glue to the back of the top section of each one. Attach the *+ heat* flaps over the top of the *Solid, Liquid, Gas* piece to show heat being added to each state to change it to the next. Repeat with the *+ cold* flaps below the piece. Under each flap, write the vocabulary word to explain each process. (solid plus heat is melting, liquid plus heat is evaporation, gas plus cold is condensation, liquid plus cold equals freezing)

6. Cut out the *Water that evaporates* flap book. Cut on the solid lines to create four flaps. Apply glue to the back of the left section and attach it to the bottom of the page. Fold the flaps in on the dashed lines to cover the blanks.

7. Fill in the blanks with the missing word.

Reflect on Learning

To complete the left-hand page, have students use the words *melt, freeze, evaporate,* and *condense* in a paragraph to explain the changing states of matter.

Changing States of Matter

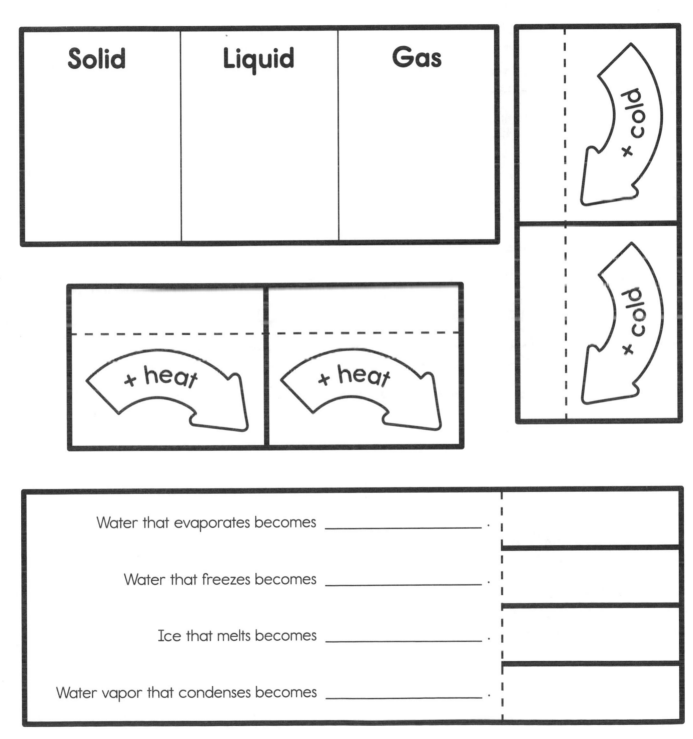

Solid	Liquid	Gas

+ heat   + heat

+ cold

+ cold

Water that evaporates becomes _____ .

Water that freezes becomes _____ .

Ice that melts becomes _____ .

Water vapor that condenses becomes _____ .

Temperature

Introduction

Discuss what the temperature is today. Ask whether it is cold or hot. Demonstrate how to use a thermometer to measure the temperature. Discuss that the two common units temperature is measured in are called Celsius and Fahrenheit.

Creating the Notebook Page

Guide students through the following steps to complete the right-hand page in their notebooks.

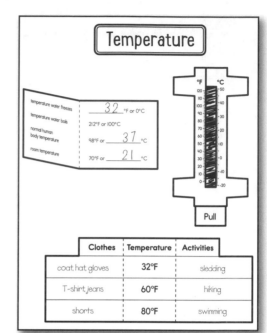

1. Add a Table of Contents entry for the Temperature pages.

2. Cut out the title and glue it to the top of the page.

3. Cut out the thermometer. Starting near the °F, cut straight down and follow the solid line to remove the center of the thermometer. Apply glue to the back of the four tabs and the very top of the thermometer. Attach the thermometer below and to the right of the title.

4. Cut out the *Pull* strip. Color it red. Slip the red strip inside the thermometer with the *Pull* near the bottom.

5. Cut out the *temperature water freezes* piece. Fold it on the dashed lines so the text is inside. Apply glue to the back of the right side and attach it to the left of the thermometer. Cut out the *Common Temperatures* piece and glue it to the front of the book.

6. Using the thermometer, write in the missing answers.

7. Cut out the *Clothes/Temperature/Activities* piece. Apply glue to the back of the middle section and attach it to the bottom of the page.

8. Fill in clothes and activities that fit each temperature. Under each flap, describe how the temperature can affect the choice of clothing and activity.

Reflect on Learning

To complete the left-hand page, write the following temperatures on the board: 60°F, 0°C, 0°F, 14°C, 60°C. Have students put them in order from coldest to warmest. Then, have students choose one of the temperatures and draw a picture to illustrate what activity she would do and what kind of clothing she would wear in that type of temperature.

Answer Key
Temperature water freezes: 32°F; Normal human body temperature: 37°C; Room temperature: 21°C

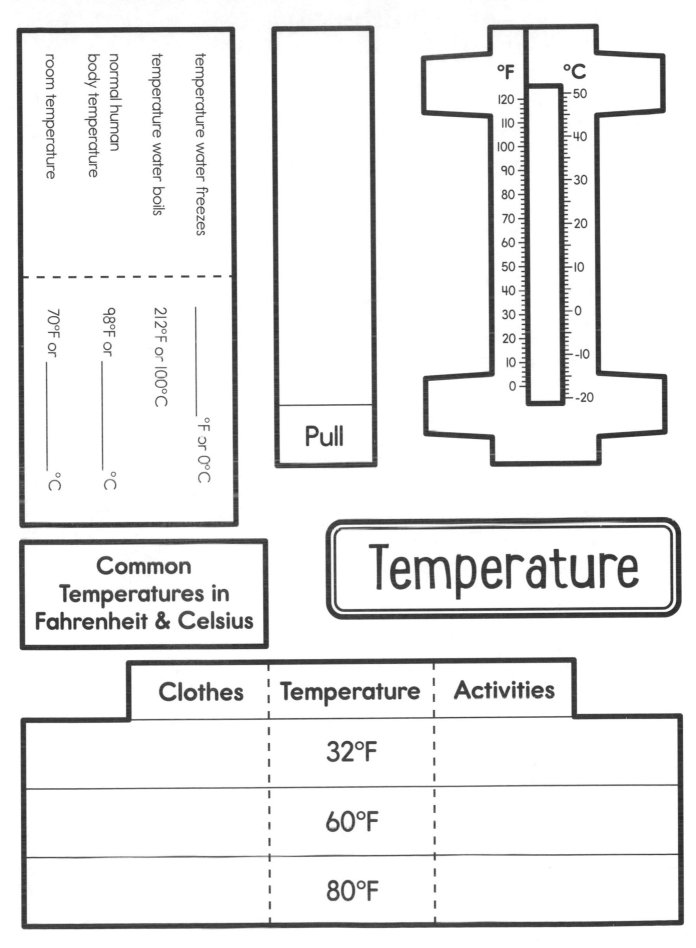

temperature water freezes

temperature water boils

normal human
body temperature

room temperature

_____ °F or 0°C

212°F or 100°C

98°F or _____ °C

70°F or _____ °C

Pull

°F   °C

120 — — 50
110 —
100 — — 40
90 —
80 — — 30
70 —
60 — — 20
50 —
40 — — 10
30 —
20 — — 0
10 —
0 — — -10

— -20

Common Temperatures in Fahrenheit & Celsius

Temperature

Clothes	Temperature	Activities
	32°F	
	60°F	
	80°F	

Energy

Each student will need a sharpened pencil and a paper clip to complete the spinner activity.

Introduction

Display a flashlight. Explain that you will be talking about different forms of energy today. Turn on the flashlight. Ask students what kind of energy a flashlight is (light energy). Have students look outside an open window. Ask what kind of energy we get from the sun (light and heat energy). Have students clap their hands. Ask what kind of energy this is an example of (sound energy). Last, have students rub their hands together. Ask whether their hands feel warm. Explain that they have created heat energy.

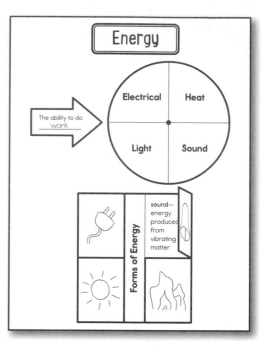

Creating the Notebook Page

Guide students through the following steps to complete the right-hand page in their notebooks.

1. Add a Table of Contents entry for the Energy pages.

2. Cut out the title and glue it to the top of the page.

3. Cut out the arrow and glue it below the title to the left.

4. Complete the definition of energy (the ability to do **work**).

5. Cut out the circle and glue it below the title to the right of the arrow.

6. Cut out the *Forms of Energy* flap book. Cut on the solid lines to create four flaps. Fold the flaps in on the dashed lines so that the definitions are covered. Apply glue to the back of the center section and attach it below the spinner.

7. On the front of each flap, draw a picture of an example of that type of energy. Then, write a real-life example of that form of energy in the blank flap.

8. Use a sharpened pencil and a paper clip to spin the spinner. Whatever energy form it lands on, point to the correct picture. Check whether you are right by opening the flap.

Reflect on Learning

To complete the left-hand page, have students give an example of something that uses both sound and light energy. Students should explain how it uses both types of energy.

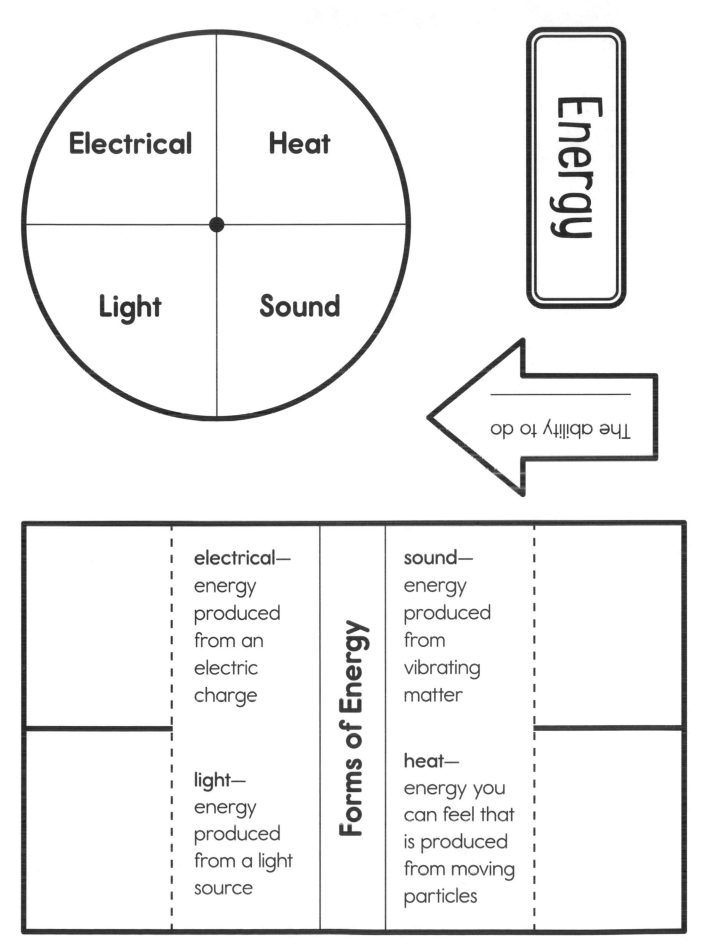

Electrical

Heat

Light

Sound

Energy

The ability to do _____

electrical—
energy
produced
from an
electric
charge

light—
energy
produced
from a light
source

Forms of Energy

sound—
energy
produced
from
vibrating
matter

heat—
energy you
can feel that
is produced
from moving
particles

Force and Motion

Introduction

Crumple a piece of scrap paper into a ball. Have a volunteer toss it lightly. Then, have another volunteer throw it with more force. Ask what the difference was between the two throws. Explain that the second time, more force was applied. Next, have students crumple pieces of scrap paper into balls. Have students show different ways to move a ball, such as dropping it, blowing on it, or hitting it with their hands. Explain that these are examples of types of motion. Objects move in many different ways.

Creating the Notebook Page

Guide students through the following steps to complete the right-hand page in their notebooks.

1. Add a Table of Contents entry for the Force and Motion pages.

2. Cut out the title and glue it to the top of the page.

3. Cut out the four-box square. Cut on the solid line to create two flaps. Fold down the top two sections. Then, fold the left side over the right. Apply glue to the back of the *can be moved from a distance* square and attach it below the title.

4. Write *Many Motions* on the top square. Complete each box with an example that fits the description.

5. Cut out the two pockets. Apply glue to the back of the tabs and attach them below the *Many Motions* book.

6. Cut out the nine objects and actions pieces.

7. Write the name of another thing that can be pushed or pulled on the blank piece. Sort the nine pieces into the correct pockets. Some pieces may have more than one correct answer.

8. At the bottom of the page, write a sentence using the words *push* and *pull* to describe a change in an object's motion.

Reflect on Learning

To complete the left-hand page, have students write a paragraph about three objects in their life that move in some way. Students' paragraphs should include descriptions of how each object moves (for example, *I slide my book into my book bag*).

Force and Motion

Objects can move in different ways.

slide	move in one direction
spin	move in more than one direction
more slowly	can be moved from a distance
more quickly	can only move when touched

Things You Push

Things You Pull

a shopping cart	bat hitting a ball	opening an oven door
a wagon	throwing a ball	removing the lid to yogurt
a swing	kicking a soccer ball	

Sound

Introduction

Review the terms *pitch* and *volume*. To demonstrate high and low pitch, place a ruler so part of it hangs off the edge of a desk or table. Pressing the ruler down firmly on the end of the desk, strum the end in the air. Demonstrate how, as the end hanging off of the desk gets shorter, the pitch gets higher. Slide the ruler back and forth while strumming the end at different lengths.

Creating the Notebook Page

Guide students through the following steps to complete the right-hand page in their notebooks.

1. Add a Table of Contents entry for the Sound pages.

2. Cut out the title and glue it to the top of the page.

3. Below the title, write and draw to describe how sound travels.

4. Cut out the four-box square and fold on the dashed line. Apply glue to the back of the bottom half and attach it below the title.

5. Fill in each box with a sound that fits the description: a low soft sound, a low loud sound, a high soft sound, and a high loud sound. On the outside, write *Sounds Can Be Different*.

6. Cut out the two blank rectangles. Fold each rectangle on the dashed lines. Fold the piece with the gray glue section so that it is inside the fold. Apply glue to the gray glue section and place the other folded rectangle on top so that the folds are nested and create a book with four cascading flaps. Make sure that the inside pages are facing up so that the edges of both pages are visible. Apply glue to the back of the book and attach it to the bottom of the page.

7. Label the top of the booklet *Sound Vocabulary*. Then, label the next flap *vibration*, the next *pitch*, and the last *loudness*.

8. Cut out the three definitions. Glue them on the appropriate pages in the *Sound Vocabulary* book. Draw a picture to match each definition.

Reflect on Learning

To complete the left-hand page, have students write the following sentences: *My favorite sound is _____. It has a (high/low) pitch and a (soft/loud) sound.* Have students complete the sentences and draw matching pictures.

	Soft	Loud
Low		
High		

Sound

how low or high a sound is
how soft or loud a sound is
a small back and forth motion

glue

Magnets

Each student will need two brass paper fasteners to complete this page.

Introduction

Give each student a small magnetic or nonmagnetic object. Distribute a variety of magnets to students. Have students test their objects to see if they are magnetic. Discuss what kinds of items stick to the magnets and why.

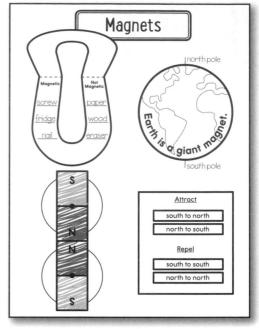

Creating the Notebook Page

Guide students through the following steps to complete the right-hand page in their notebooks.

1. Add a Table of Contents entry for the Magnets pages.

2. Cut out the title and glue it to the top of the page.

3. Cut out the horseshoe magnet. Fold on the dashed line so that the text is showing. Cut out the middle on the solid line. Fold the piece the other way so the text is on the inside. Apply glue to the back of the piece and attach it to the page below and to the left of the title. Write examples of objects that are magnetic and not magnetic on the lines.

4. Cut out the Earth piece. Glue it next to the horseshoe magnet. Discuss what makes Earth a magnet. Then, draw the North and South poles on the picture. Label them.

5. Cut out the two bar magnets and the two gray circles. Color-code the sides of each magnet.

6. Push a brass paper fastener into the center of one of the bar magnets and then through the center of one of the two gray circles with the white side facing up. It may be helpful to create a hole in each piece separately first. Apply glue to the gray side of the circle and attach it below the horseshoe magnet. The brass paper fastener should not go through the page and the circle should spin freely. Repeat with the second bar magnet and circle, attaching it below the other magnet so that the magnets' north and south poles will touch when spun.

7. Cut out the *Attract/Repel* piece. Glue it next to the bar magnets.

8. Cut out the four *north to south* pieces. Spin the two bar magnets to model the situation on each piece. Decide if the magnets would attract or repel. Glue the piece onto the *Attract/Repel* chart below the correct heading.

Reflect on Learning

To complete the left-hand page, have students trace their hands. In each finger, have students write one fact about magnets.

© Carson-Dellosa • CD-104906

Magnets

Magnetic | Not Magnetic

_____ | _____

_____ | _____

_____ | _____

glue

glue

S

N

| north to north |
| south to south |
| north to south |
| south to north |

N ● S

Attract

Repel

Earth is a giant magnet.

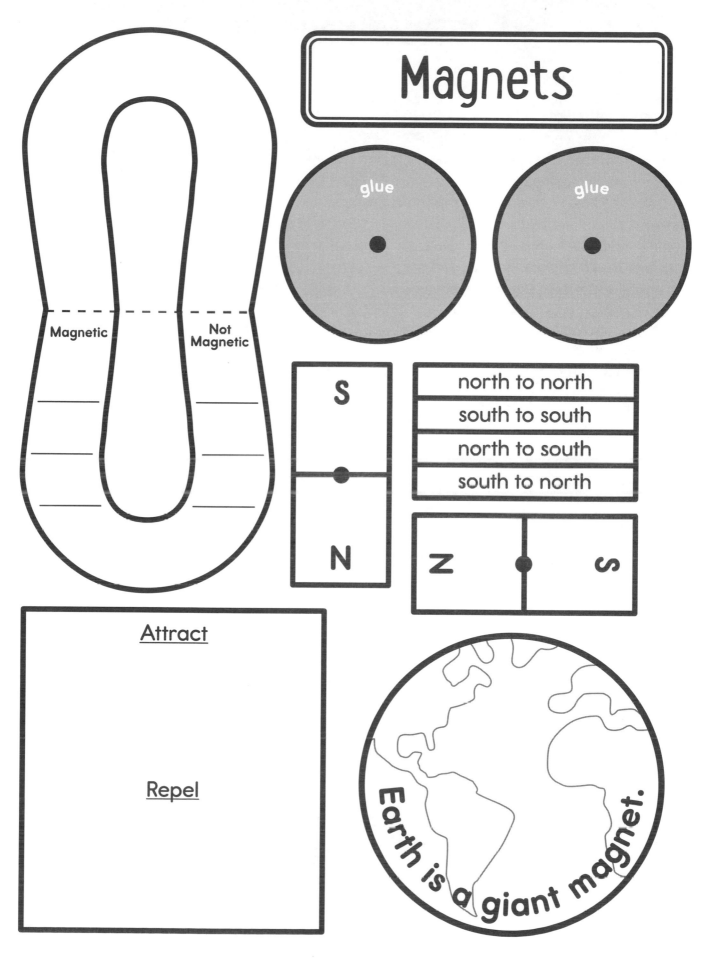

Earth's Resources

Introduction

Set out a variety of items that come from natural resources, such as a pencil, paper, and an apple. Hold up each item and ask students where we get the parts. Explain that items that come directly from rocks, minerals, water, plants, and animals are called natural resources. Items that are made by humans are considered man-made. Many man-made items, such as the pencil, are made from natural resources such as wood and graphite.

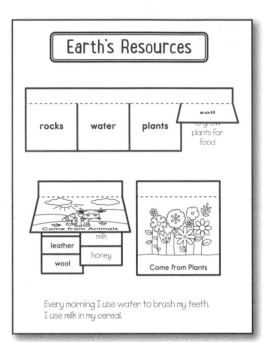

Creating the Notebook Page

Guide students through the following steps to complete the right-hand page in their notebooks.

1. Add a Table of Contents entry for the Earth's Resources pages.

2. Cut out the title and glue it to the top of the page.

3. Cut out the *rocks* flap book. Cut on the solid lines to create four flaps. Apply glue to the back of the top section and attach it below the title.

4. Under each flap, write or draw how we use each of the natural resources.

5. Cut out the *Come from* flaps. Apply glue to the back of the top of both pieces and attach them to the bottom of the page.

6. Cut out the resource pieces. Write in three more resources on the blank pieces. Glue them under the correct flaps.

7. On the bottom of the page, write a sentence describing how you use natural resources in your everyday life.

Reflect on Learning

To complete the left-hand page, write a list on the board of objects and materials such as *plastic, coal, egg, basketball,* and *honey.* Have students create a T-chart labeled *Natural* or *Man-made* and write the items under the correct heading. Then, have them add two objects of their choosing under each heading.

Answer Key
Comes from Plants: cotton, paper, salad, wood; Comes from Animals: eggs, leather, wool

Earth's Resources

rocks	water	plants	soil

Come from Animals

Come from Plants

cotton	leather	paper	salad	eggs
wood	wool			

Landforms

Introduction

Distribute a handful of play dough or modeling clay to students or small groups of students. Have them create small models of each landform as you say them: mountain, valley, volcano, river, and hill. Ask students to explain the difference between the mountain and the volcano, as well as between the mountain and the hill.

Creating the Notebook Page

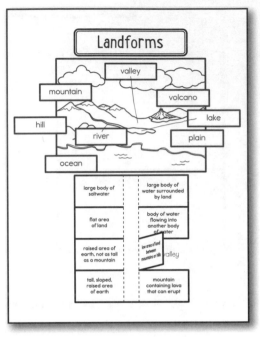

Guide students through the following steps to complete the right-hand page in their notebooks.

1. Add a Table of Contents entry for the Landforms pages.

2. Cut out the title and glue it to the top of the page.

3. Cut out the landforms picture. Glue it below the title.

4. Cut out the definitions flap book. Cut on the solid lines to create eight flaps. Apply glue to the back of the center section and attach it below the landforms picture.

5. Cut out the eight landform words.

6. Read each flap. Find the matching word and glue it to the correct landform on the picture. Or, glue it near the landform and draw a line from the label to the landform. Then, write the word under the flap.

Reflect on Learning

To complete the left-hand page, have each student draw a picture of the state she lives in and label the major landforms. Or, provide a copy of a physical map for students to glue into their notebooks and label appropriately.

Answer Key
large body of saltwater: ocean; flat area of land: plain; raised area of earth, not as tall as a mountain: hill; tall, sloped raised area of earth: mountain; large body of water surrounded by land: lake; body of water flowing into another body of water: river; low area of land between mountains or hills: valley; mountain containing lava that can erupt: volcano

Landforms

large body of saltwater	large body of water surrounded by land
flat area of land	body of water flowing into another body of water
raised area of earth, not as tall as a mountain	low area of land between mountains or hills
tall, sloped, raised area of earth	mountain containing lava that can erupt

plain	ocean
valley	mountain
volcano	hill
lake	river

Soil

Introduction

Bring in three glass or plastic containers—one with marbles, one with clay, and one with flour and some water in an additional container. Explain that the marbles are similar to sandy soil. Ask what would happen if you poured water over the marbles (it would quickly drain through). Demonstrate. Hold up the container with clay in it. Ask what would happen if you poured water over the clay (the water would stay on the clay and not drain through). Demonstrate. Show the container of flour. Ask what might be a problem with this type of "soil" when it hasn't gotten a lot of water (the fine dust blows away). Explain that a mix of all three is ideal. This type of soil is called loam.

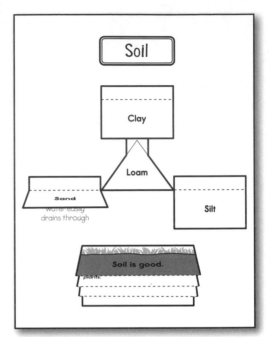

Creating the Notebook Page

Guide students through the following steps to complete the right-hand page in their notebooks.

1. Add a Table of Contents entry for the Soil pages.

2. Cut out the title and glue it to the top of the page.

3. Cut out the *Loam* piece. Apply glue to the back of the top section and attach it below the title, leaving space above it for one of the rectangular flaps.

4. Cut out the *Sand, Clay,* and *Silt* flaps. Apply glue to the top section of each and attach one next to each corner of the loam triangle. Attach the remaining flap above the loam triangle.

5. Under each of the four flaps, write a description of that type of soil.

6. Cut out the *Soil is* accordion fold. Fold on the dashed lines to make an accordion fold with the blank section in the back. Apply glue to the back of the blank section and attach it to the bottom of the page.

7. Draw a picture or give more information next to each sentence. In the blank section, add another use for soil.

Reflect on Learning

To complete the left-hand page, have students write a recipe for making the perfect soil for a mud pie. Students should explain why they chose to include the type(s) of soil(s) that they used in their recipes.

© Carson-Dellosa • CD-104906

Soil is good.

It gives animals homes.

It supports and nourishes plants.

It holds water.

It cleans water.

It absorbs gases and dirt.

Soil

Loam

Sand

Clay

Silt

Daily and Seasonal Changes

Introduction

Write the names of various seasonal changes on index cards, such as *Baby birds are born*, *Trees lose their leaves*, *Animals hibernate*, and *Trees get buds*. Distribute one card to each student. Designate a corner of the room to each season and post a sign. Have students go to the corner their card best fits. Starting with one season, have students in that corner read off all of the events that occur in that season. Repeat with the other three seasons.

Creating the Notebook Page

Guide students through the following steps to complete the right-hand page in their notebooks.

1. Add a Table of Contents entry for the Daily and Seasonal Changes pages.

2. Cut out the title and glue it to the top of the page.

3. Cut out the *day* and *night* flaps. Apply glue to the gray glue section of the *night* flap and place the *day* flap on top to create a stacked, two-flap book. Apply glue to the back of the top section and attach it below the title to the left.

4. On each flap, draw things you would see in the day or at night. Include animals, changes to plants, and things in the sky. Under the bottom flap, write a sentence telling how night and day are different. Next to the book, write a sentence to tell what makes day become night.

5. Cut out the four seasons flaps. Apply glue to the gray glue section of the *winter* flap and place the *autumn* flap on top. Repeat with the *summer* and *spring* flaps to create a four-flap stacked book. Apply glue to the back of the top section of the stacked book and attach it to the page.

6. On each page, complete the tree to look as it would in each season. Draw other things that happen during that season. Under the bottom flap, write a sentence to tell how the seasons are different. Below the seasons book, write a sentence to tell what causes the changing seasons.

Reflect on Learning

To complete the left-hand page, have students write a poem about the changes that happen to a tree through each of the four seasons. Allow time for students to share their work.

Daily and Seasonal Changes

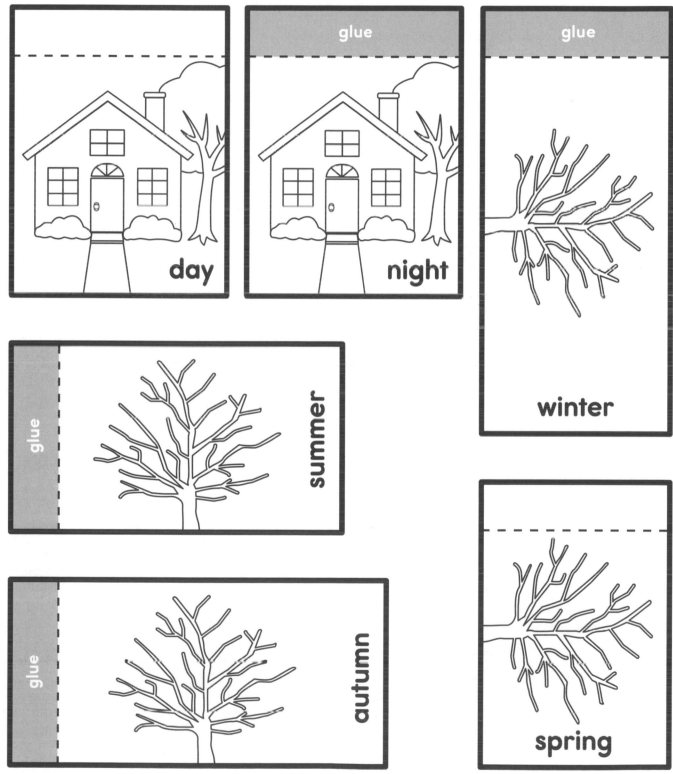

day

night

winter

summer

autumn

spring

The Moon

Introduction

Ask whether students saw the moon last night or today. Have a volunteer come to the board and draw what it looked like. Explain how the sun illuminates the moon. Using a small ball and a flashlight in a darkened room, demonstrate how and why we see the different phases of the moon.

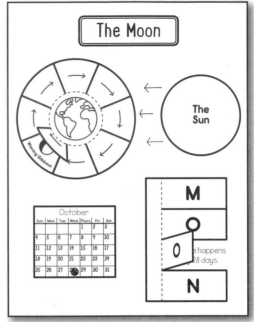

Creating the Notebook Page

Guide students through the following steps to complete the right-hand page in their notebooks.

1. Add a Table of Contents entry for The Moon pages.

2. Cut out the title and glue it to the top of the page.

3. Cut out the moon phases circle. Cut on the solid lines to create eight flaps. Apply glue to the back of the center section and attach it below and to the left of the title with the *First Quarter* moon at the top.

4. Cut out the Earth circle. Cut on the solid lines to create eight flaps. Apply glue to the gray glue section of the moon phases circle. Place the Earth piece on top, aligning the pictures with the flaps.

5. Cut out *The Sun* piece and glue it to the right of the earth and moon piece.

6. Draw lines from the sun representing the sun's rays. Open each flap to see what the moon would look like in different stages of its cycle. Use the moon flaps to lift up each moon and see its position relative to the sun and how that creates the phase. Discuss the different stages with a partner.

7. Cut out the calendar piece and glue it below the Earth and moon pieces. Fill in the dates for the current month. Find out when the full moon is and draw it on the calendar.

8. Cut out the *MOON* flap book. Cut on the solid lines to create four flaps. Apply glue to the back of the left section and attach it to the page.

9. Under each flap, write one fact about the moon beginning with that letter.

Reflect on Learning

To complete the left-hand page, draw a picture on the board of the sun on the left-hand side, then Earth, then a blank circle for the moon. Have students draw what the moon would look like in this situation. Explain and tell what the phase is called.

First Quarter

Waxing Gibbous

Waxing Crescent

Waning Gibbous

Full Moon

glue

New Moon

Third Quarter

Waning Crescent

M
O
O
N

Sun.	Mon.	Tue.	Wed.	Thurs.	Fri.	Sat.

The Moon

The Sun

The Sun's Energy

Introduction

Write the following phrases on index cards: *a plant to grow, the earth to get hot, things to melt, water to evaporate*. Explain that the students will pick a card and act out something the sun's energy causes to happen. Have a volunteer choose a card and let the class guess what the student is demonstrating. Repeat until all of the cards have been used.

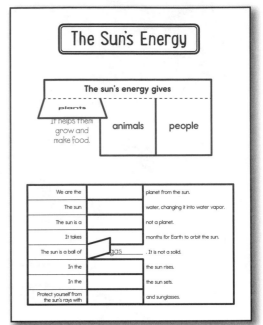

Creating the Notebook Page

Guide students through the following steps to complete the right-hand page in their notebooks.

1. Add a Table of Contents entry for The Sun's Energy pages.

2. Cut out the title and glue it to the top of the page.

3. Cut out *The sun's energy gives* flap book. Cut on the solid lines to create three flaps. Apply glue to the back of the top section and attach it below the title.

4. Under each flap, tell how the sun impacts plants, animals, and people.

5. Cut out the *We are the* piece. Glue it to the left side of the bottom of the page.

6. Cut out the large flap book. Cut on the solid lines to create eight flaps. Fold them in on the dashed line so the flaps cover the answer lines. With the paper still folded, apply glue to the back and attach it to the page next to the *We are the* piece, forming sentences with a missing word.

7. Fill in the missing words under each flap.

Reflect on Learning

To complete the left-hand page, have students plan an idea for an experiment that proves that we get energy from the sun.

Answer Key
From top to bottom: third; evaporates; star; 12; gas; morning; evening; sunscreen

The sun's energy gives

plants	animals	people

The Sun's Energy

planet from the sun.

water, changing it into water vapor.

not a planet.

months for Earth to orbit the sun.

. It is not a solid.

the sun rises.

the sun sets.

and sunglasses.

We are the
The sun
The sun is a
It takes
The sun is a ball of
In the
In the
Protect yourself from the sun's rays with

The Water Cycle

Each student will need a brass paper fastener to complete this page.

Introduction

Draw the water cycle on the board. Discuss and review the water cycle with the class. Divide the class into small groups. Have students take turns acting out one stage of the cycle and having their group guess what stage the group is representing.

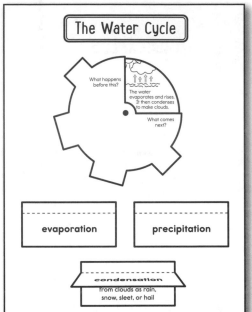

Creating the Notebook Page

Guide students through the following steps to complete the right-hand page in their notebooks.

1. Add a Table of Contents entry for The Water Cycle pages.

2. Cut out the title and glue it to the top of the page.

3. Cut out the two circles. Place the *What happens before this?* piece on top of the water cycle circle. Push a brass paper fastener through the center dots of the circles to attach them. It may be helpful to create the hole in each piece separately first. Apply glue to the back of the *What happens* piece tabs and attach it below the title. The brass paper fastener should not go through the page, and the water cycle circle should spin freely.

4. Look at each phase of the water cycle. Select one phase. Then, figure out what would happen before and after that phase. Check if you were correct by spinning the circle and viewing the phase before and after it.

5. Cut out the three flaps. Apply glue to the back of the top sections and attach them to the page below the water cycle spinner.

6. Cut out the three definitions. Glue the correct one below each flap.

Reflect on Learning

To complete the left-hand page, have each student write a story as if they were a snowflake falling from the sky. Students should describe what happens to them as they go through the complete water cycle.

Answer Key
evaporation: water changing from liquid to water vapor; precipitation: water coming down from clouds as rain, snow, sleet, or hail; condensation: water changing from water vapor to liquid, forming clouds

The Water Cycle

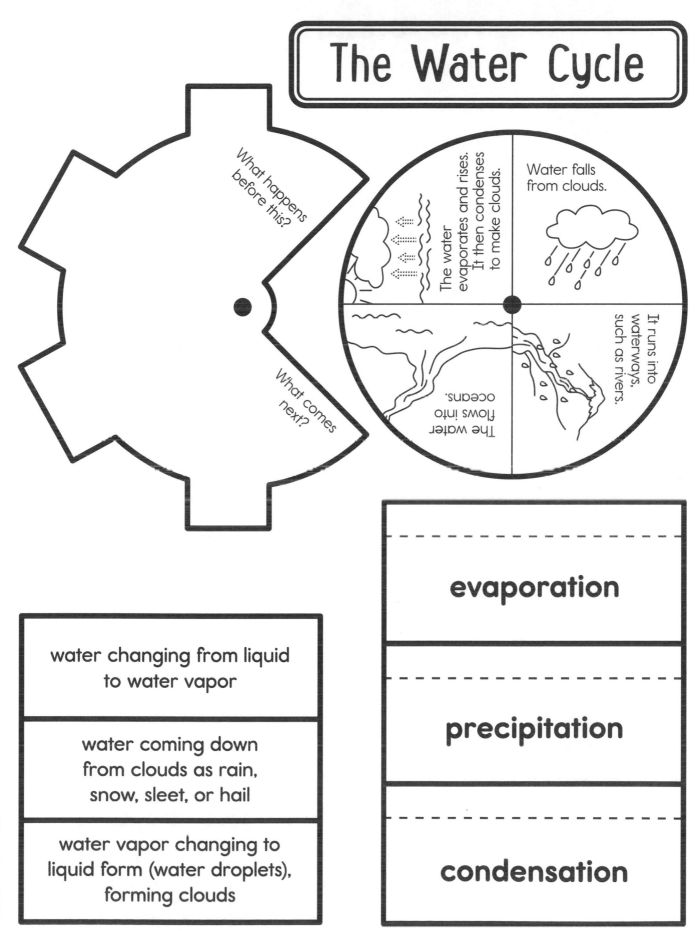

What happens before this?

What comes next?

Water falls from clouds.

The water evaporates and rises. It then condenses to make clouds.

It runs into waterways, such as rivers.

The water flows into oceans.

water changing from liquid to water vapor

water coming down from clouds as rain, snow, sleet, or hail

water vapor changing to liquid form (water droplets), forming clouds

evaporation

precipitation

condensation

Clouds

Introduction

Distribute cotton balls, blue construction paper, and glue to each student. Demonstrate how to fold the paper into thirds. Review the different cloud types. Have students create cirrus, cumulus, and stratus clouds on each third of the paper using the cotton balls and glue. Have them label each cloud type.

Creating the Notebook Page

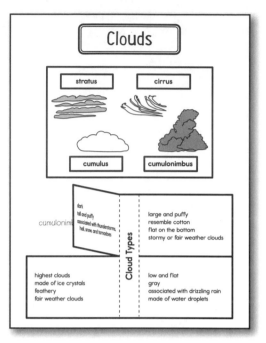

Guide students through the following steps to complete the right-hand page in their notebooks.

1.   Add a Table of Contents entry for the Clouds pages.

2.   Cut out the title and glue it to the top of the page.

3.   Cut out the cloud diagram and glue it below the title.

4.   Cut out the four cloud-name pieces. Glue the correct name to its picture.

5.   Cut out the *Cloud Types* flap book. Cut on the solid lines to create four flaps. Apply glue to the back of the center section and attach it to the bottom of the page.

6.   Under each flap, write the name of the cloud that is being described.

Reflect on Learning

To complete the left-hand page, have students draw two large overlapping circles to create a Venn diagram to compare two cloud types. Allow time for students to share their work.

Answer Key
highest clouds: cirrus; dark: cumulonimbus; large and puffy: cumulus; low and flat: stratus

Clouds

cumulonimbus	cirrus
cumulus	stratus

Cloud Types

dark
tall and puffy
associated with thunderstorms, hail, snow, and tornadoes

large and puffy
resemble cotton
flat on the bottom
stormy or fair weather clouds

highest clouds
made of ice crystals
feathery
fair weather clouds

low and flat
gray
associated with drizzling rain
made of water droplets

Human Impact on Earth

Distribute a self-stick note to each student. Have them write things humans do that either help or hurt Earth. Collect them and redistribute them so each student gets someone else's self-stick note. Draw a T-chart on the board labeled *Help Earth* and *Hurt Earth*. Have each student read their self-stick note and then place it on the board under the correct heading. As they place them on the chart, ask students to describe how plants and animals are affected by these actions.

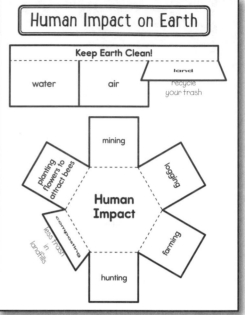

Creating the Notebook Page

Guide students through the following steps to complete the right-hand page in their notebooks.

1. Add a Table of Contents entry for the Human Impact on Earth pages.

2. Cut out the title and glue it to the top of the page.

3. Cut out the *Keep Earth Clean!* flap book. Cut on the solid lines to create three flaps. Apply glue to the back of the top section and attach it below the title.

4. Under each flap, write ways to keep the water, air, and land clear of pollution.

5. Cut out the *Human Impact* flap book. Apply glue to the back of the center section and attach it below the flap book.

6. Under each flap, write how each activity impacts the earth.

Reflect on Learning

To complete the left-hand page, have students create a poster describing three ways we can help the planet. Allow time for students to share their work.

Human Impact on Earth

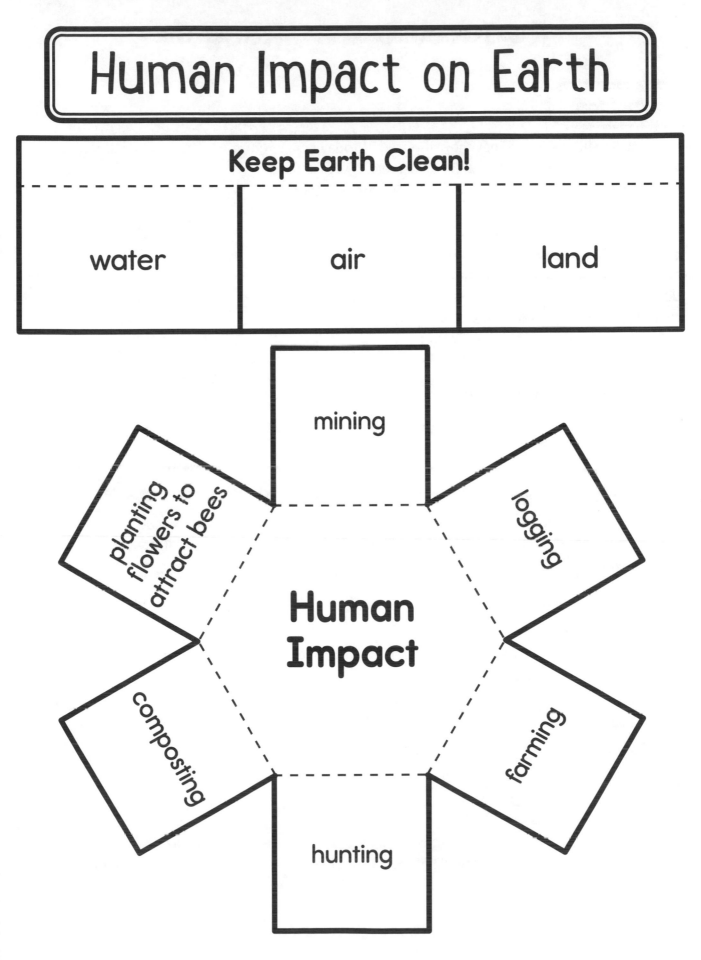

Keep Earth Clean!

water | air | land

mining

planting flowers to attract bees

logging

Human Impact

composting

farming

hunting

Reduce, Reuse, Recycle

Ask students to share some things they disposed of today (a napkin, the uneaten portion of their breakfast, etc.). Ask what happens when these items end up in the trash. Discuss other options for disposing of these items.

Creating the Notebook Page

Guide students through the following steps to complete the right-hand page in their notebooks.

1. Add a Table of Contents entry for the Reduce, Reuse, Recycle pages.

2. Cut out the title and glue it to the top of the page.

3. Cut out the *Reduce, Reuse, Recycle* triangle. Apply glue to the back of the center section and attach it below and to the left of the title.

4. Under each flap, write an example of what you can reduce, reuse, and recycle.

5. Cut out the *recycling bin, trash can*, and *compost bin* pockets. Apply glue to the back of the tabs and attach the pockets below each other along the right side of the page.

6. Cut out the object pieces. Write two more objects on the two blank pieces.

7. Decide if each piece should be recycled, composted, or go to a landfill. Place it in the correct pocket.

8. Cut out the *My Pledge to the Earth* piece. Apply glue to the back of the top section and glue it below the triangle.

9. Complete the pledge with the things you promise to do to help make Earth a good place to live. Use the space under the flap and the rest of the page if more space is needed.

Reflect on Learning

To complete the left-hand page, have students draw or cut pictures out of magazines of things that should not go into a trash can or landfill. Students should choose one item and write a sentence to explain why.

Answer Key

recycling bin: cereal box, glass pickle jar, notebook paper, plastic water bottle, tuna can; trash can: ham and cheese sandwich, plastic diaper, used paper towel; compost bin: apple core, banana peel

Reduce, Reuse, Recycle

Reuse

Recycle

Reduce

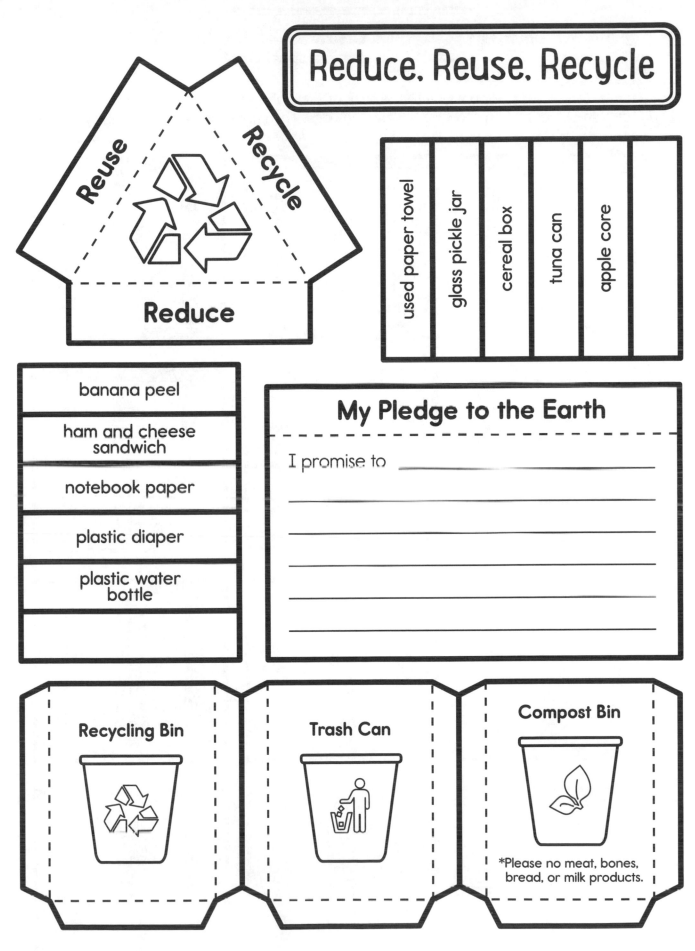

used paper towel

glass pickle jar

cereal box

tuna can

apple core

banana peel

ham and cheese sandwich

notebook paper

plastic diaper

plastic water bottle

My Pledge to the Earth

I promise to _____

_____

_____

_____

_____

Recycling Bin

Trash Can

Compost Bin

*Please no meat, bones, bread, or milk products.

Tabs

Cut out each tab and label it. Apply glue to the back of each tab and align it on the outside edge of the page with only the label section showing beyond the edge. Then, fold each tab to seal the page inside.

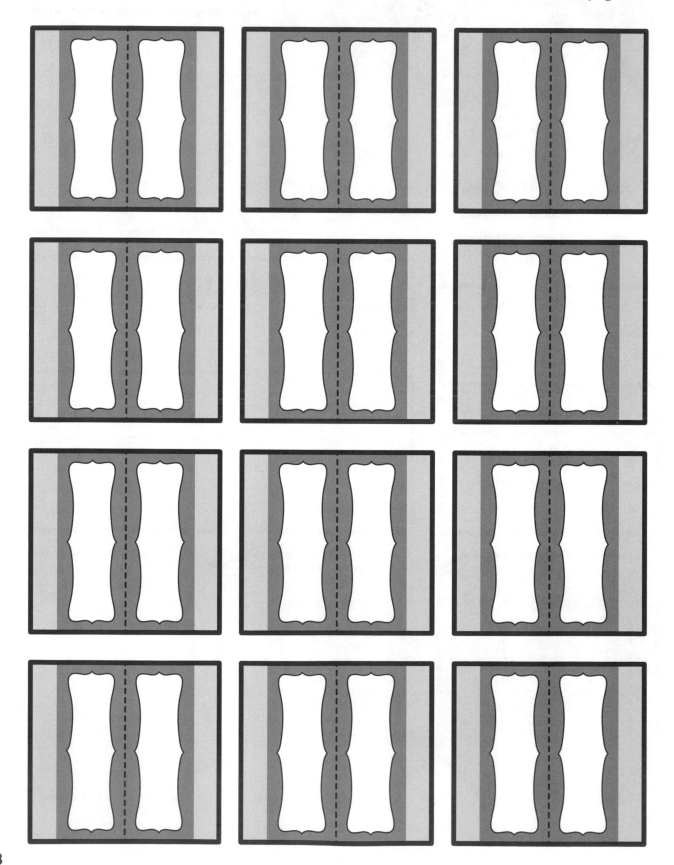

© Carson-Dellosa • CD-104906

Cut out the KWL chart and cut on the solid lines to create three separate flaps. Apply glue to the back of the Topic section to attach the chart to a notebook page.

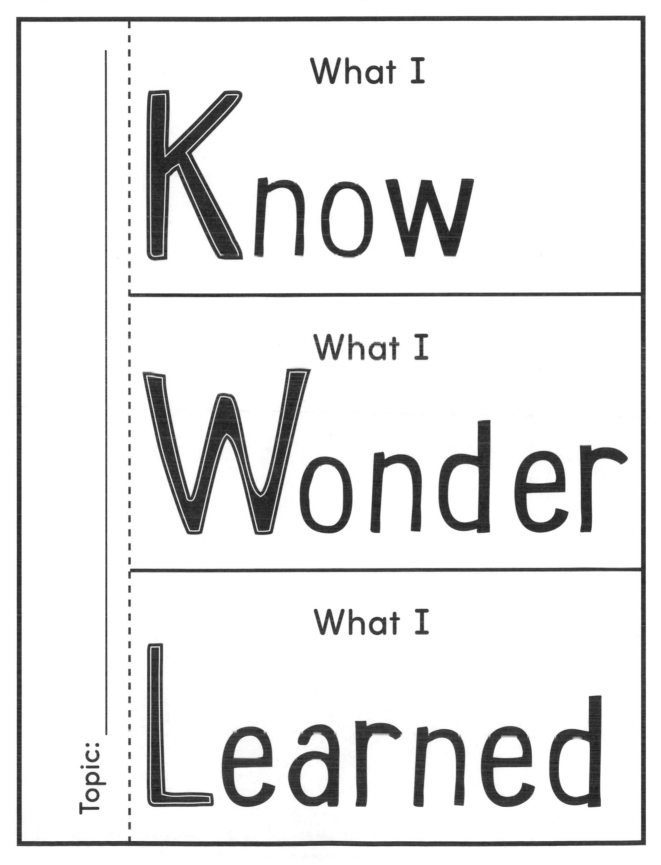

Library Pocket

Cut out the library pocket on the solid lines. Fold in the side tabs and apply glue to them before folding up the front of the pocket. Apply glue to the back of the pocket to attach it to a notebook page.

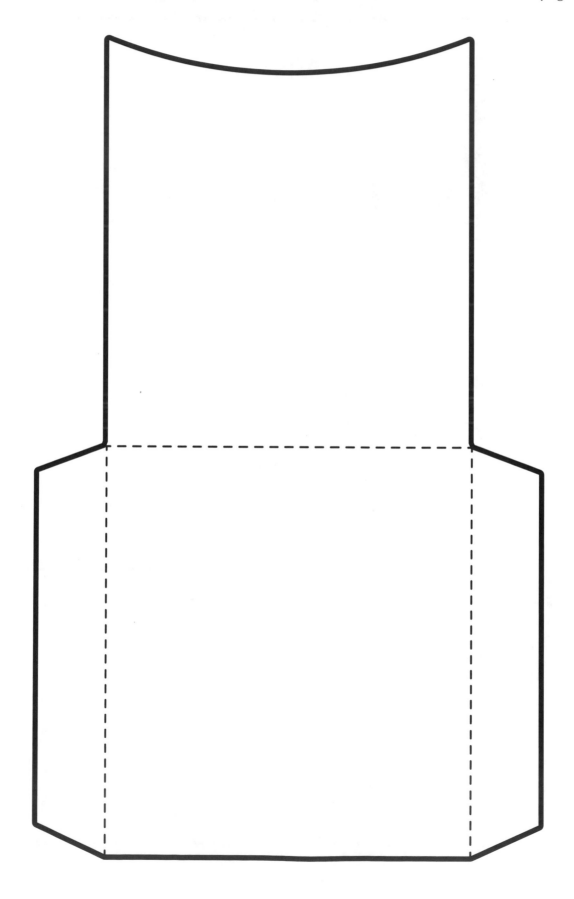

Cut out the envelope on the solid lines. Fold in the side tabs and apply glue to them before folding up the rectangular front of the envelope. Fold down the triangular flap to close the envelope. Apply glue to the back of the envelope to attach it to a notebook page.

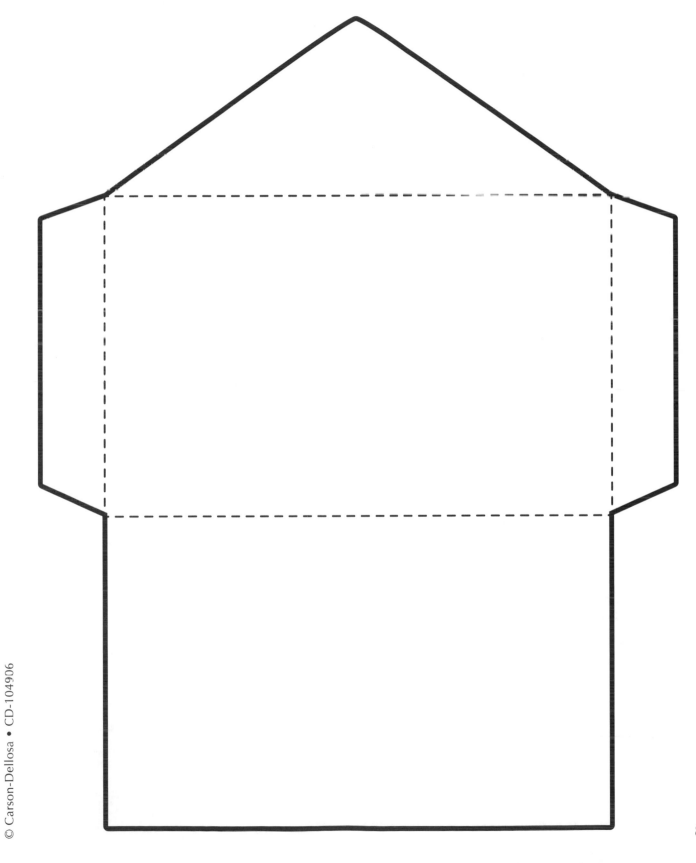

Pocket and Cards

Cut out the pocket on the solid lines. Fold over the front of the pocket. Then, apply glue to the tabs and fold them around the back of the pocket. Apply glue to the back of the pocket to attach it to a notebook page. Cut out the cards and store them in the envelope.

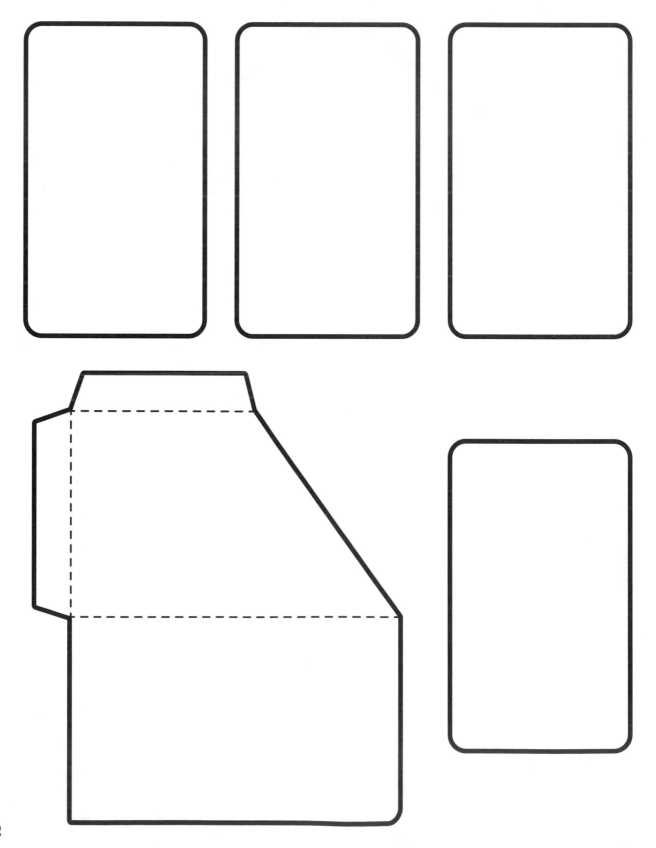

Six-Flap Shutter Fold

Cut out the shutter fold around the outside border. Then, cut on the solid lines to create six flaps. Fold the flaps toward the center. Apply glue to the back of the shutter fold to attach it to a notebook page.

If desired, this template can be modified to create a four-flap shutter fold by cutting off the bottom row. You can also create two three-flap books by cutting it in half down the center line.

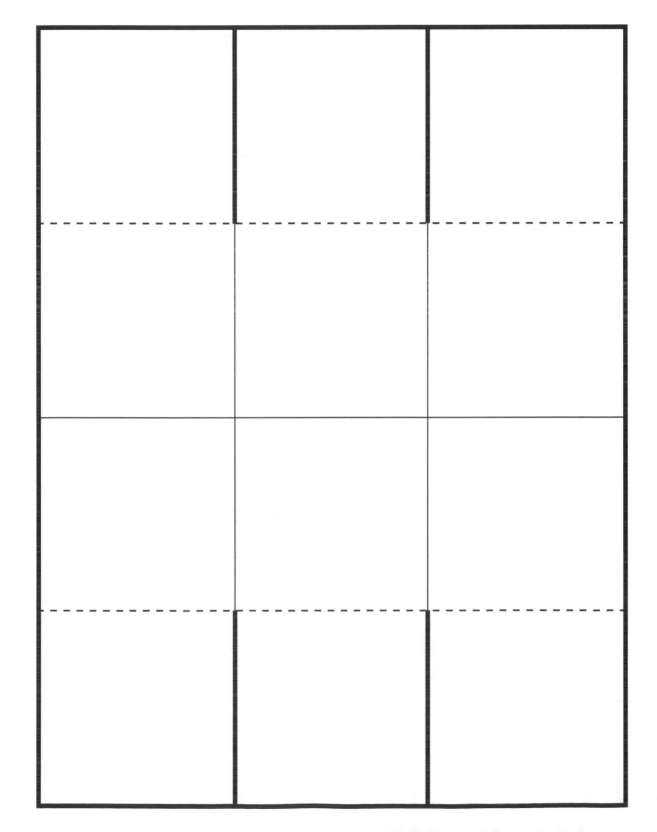

Eight-Flap Shutter Fold

Cut out the shutter fold around the outside border. Then, cut on the solid lines to create eight flaps. Fold the flaps toward the center. Apply glue to the back of the shutter fold to attach it to a notebook page.

If desired, this template can be modified to create two four-flap shutter folds by cutting off the bottom two rows. You can also create two four-flap books by cutting it in half down the center line.

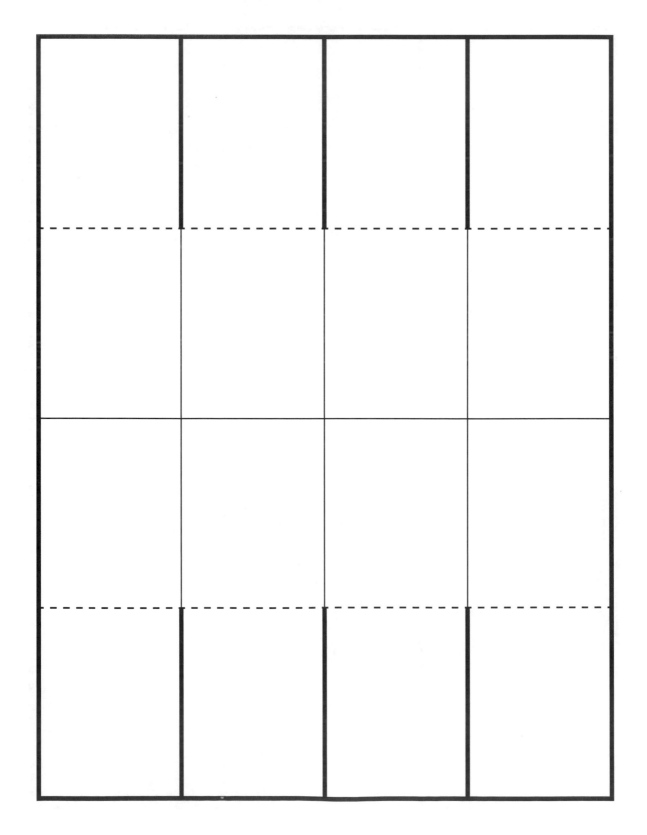

Flap Book—Eight Flaps

Cut out the flap book around the outside border. Then, cut on the solid lines to create eight flaps. Apply glue to the back of the center section to attach it to a notebook page.

If desired, this template can be modified to create a six-flap or two four-flap books by cutting off the bottom row or two. You can also create a tall four-flap book by cutting off the flaps on the left side.

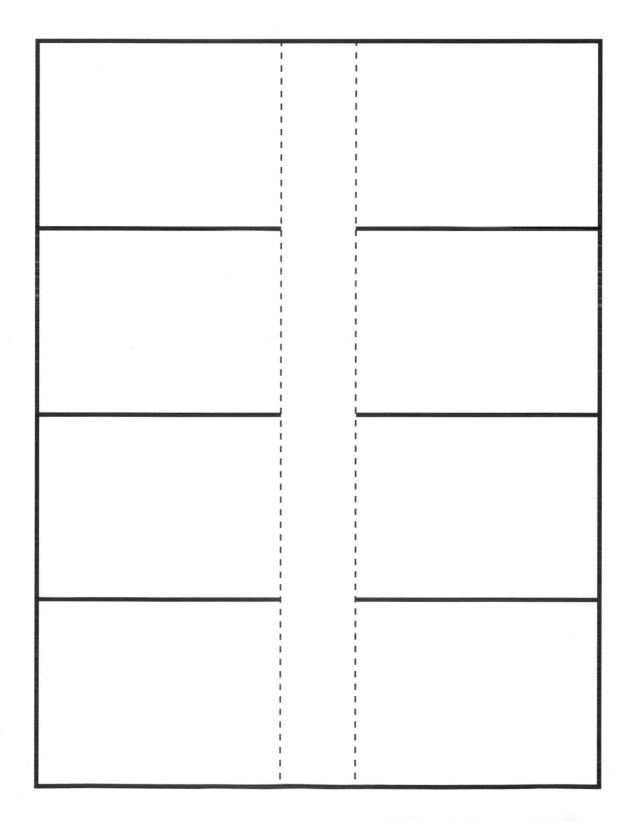

Flap Book—Twelve Flaps

Cut out the flap book around the outside border. Then, cut on the solid lines to create 12 flaps. Apply glue to the back of the center section to attach it to a notebook page.

If desired, this template can be modified to create smaller flap books by cutting off any number of rows from the bottom. You can also create a tall flap book by cutting off the flaps on the left side.

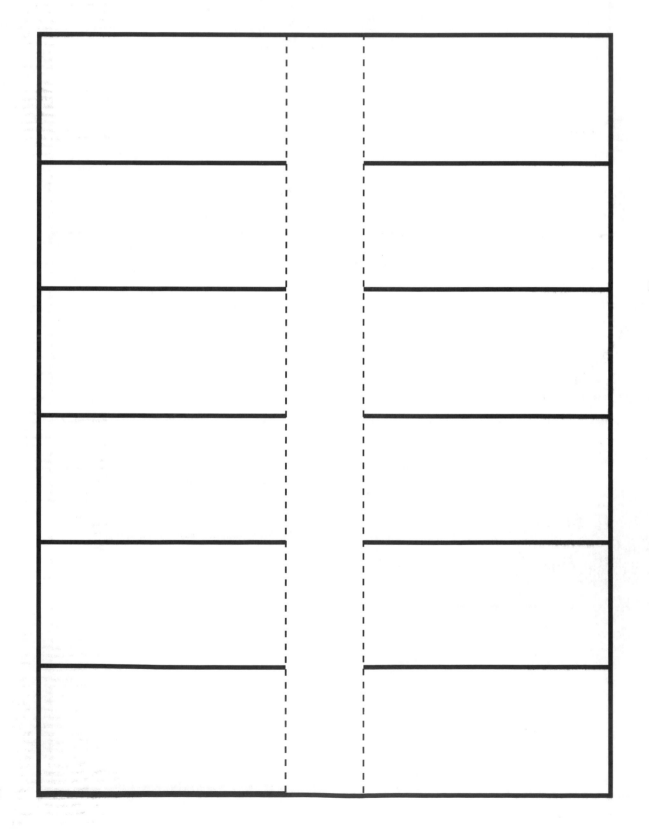

Shaped Flaps

Cut out each shaped flap. Apply glue to the back of the narrow section to attach it to a notebook page.

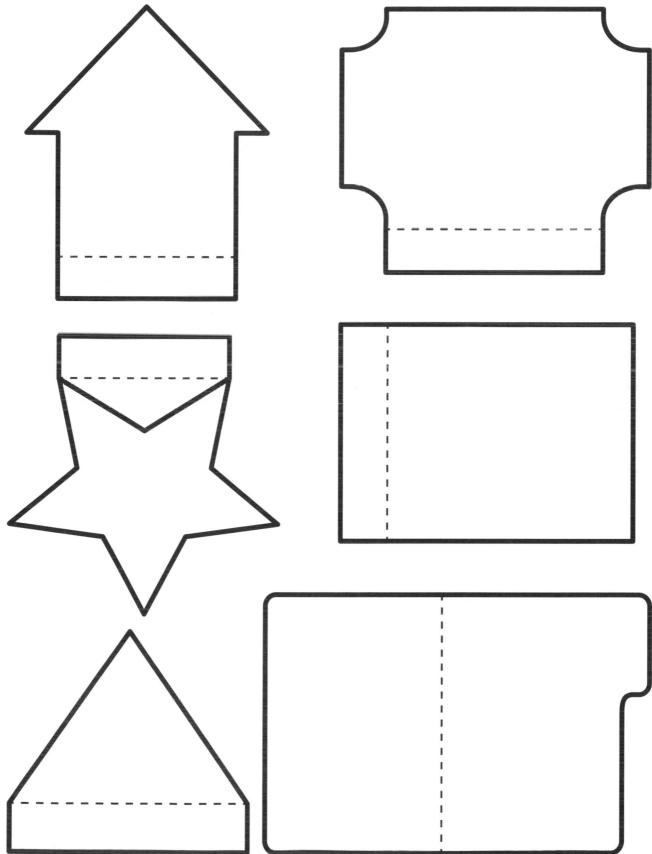

Shaped Flaps

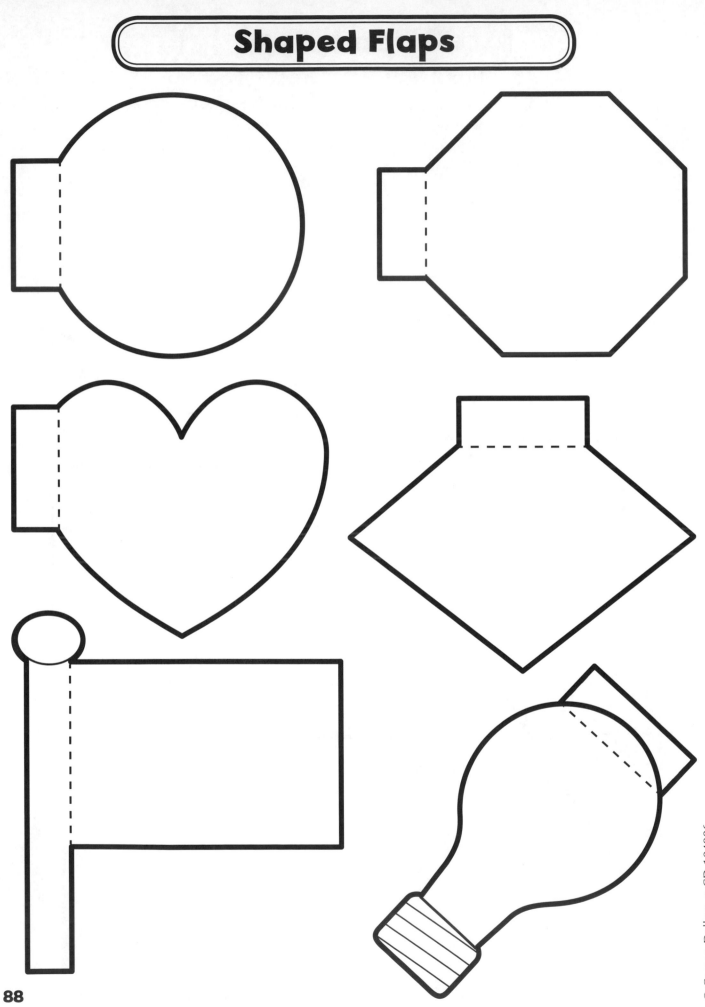

Interlocking Booklet

Cut out the booklet on the solid lines, including the short vertical lines on the top and bottom flaps. Then, fold the top and bottom flaps toward the center, interlocking them using the small vertical cuts. Apply glue to the back of the center panel to attach it to a notebook page.

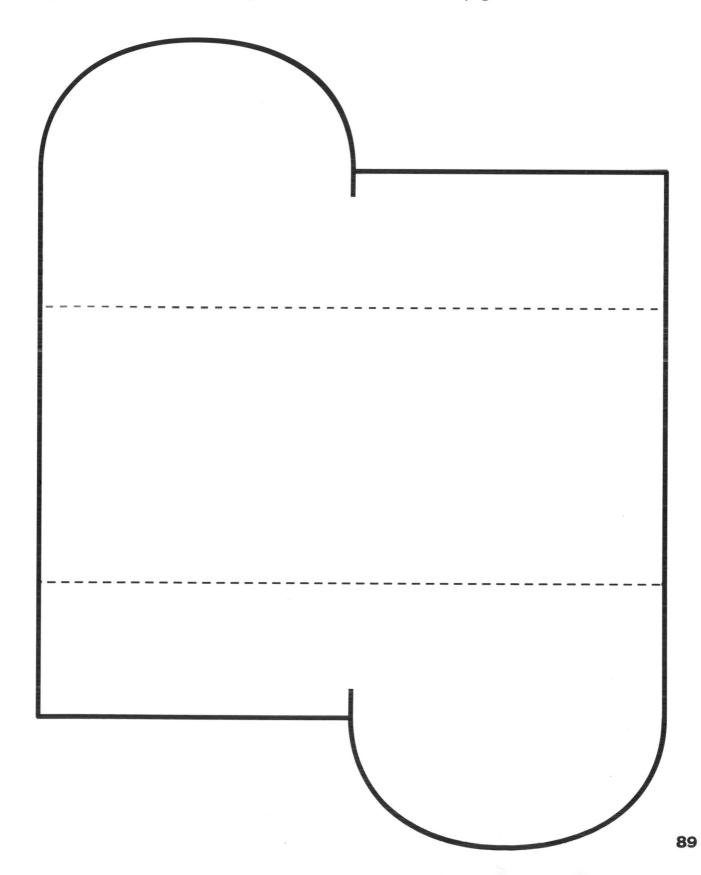

Cut out the shape on the solid lines. Then, fold the flaps toward the center. Apply glue to the back of the center panel to attach it to a notebook page.

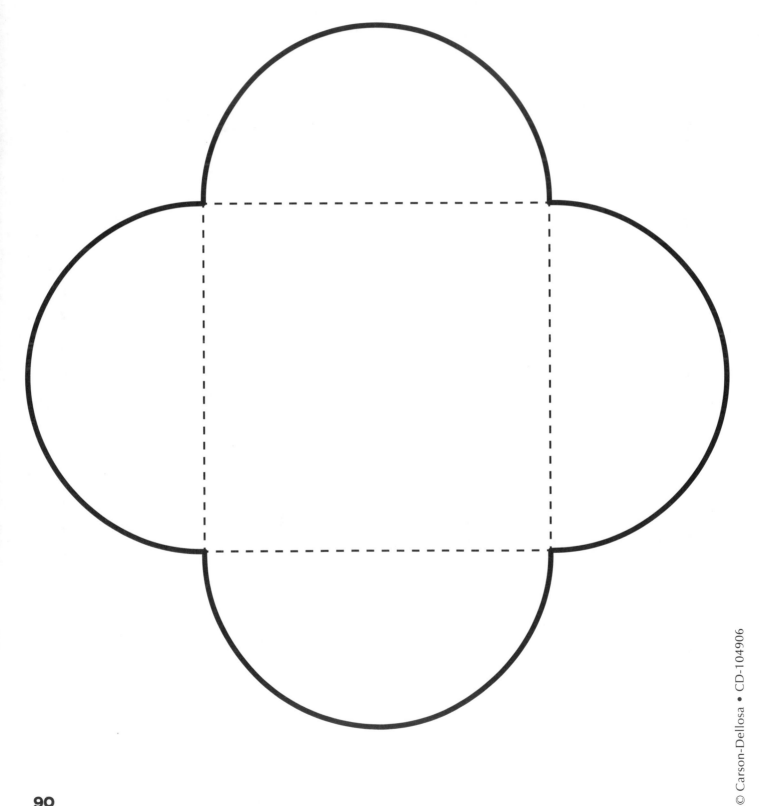

Six-Flap Petal Fold

Cut out the shape on the solid lines. Then, fold the flaps toward the center and back out. Apply glue to the back of the center panel to attach it to a notebook page.

Accordion Folds

Cut out the accordion pieces on the solid lines. Fold on the dashed lines, alternating the fold direction. Apply glue to the back of the last section to attach it to a notebook page.

You may modify the accordion books to have more or fewer pages by cutting off extra pages or by having students glue the first and last panels of two accordion books together.

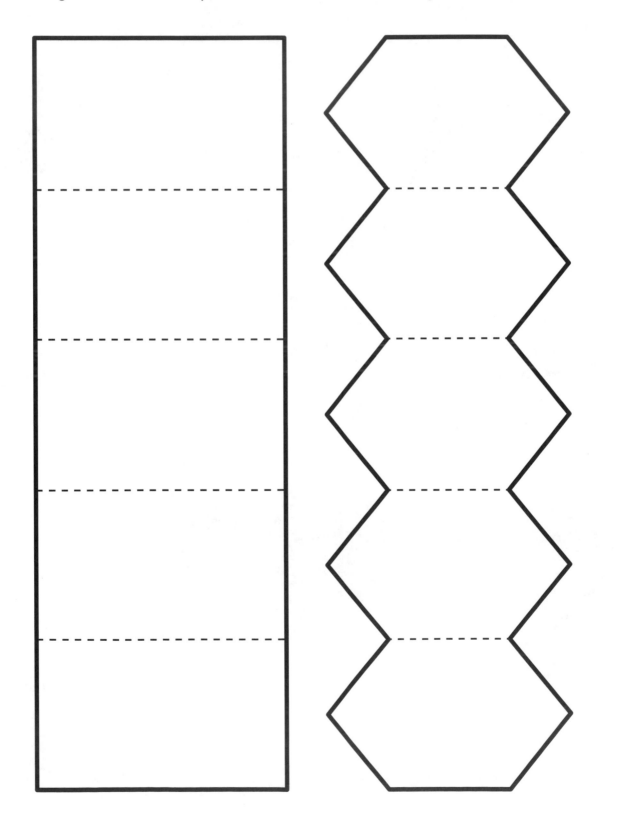

Accordion Folds

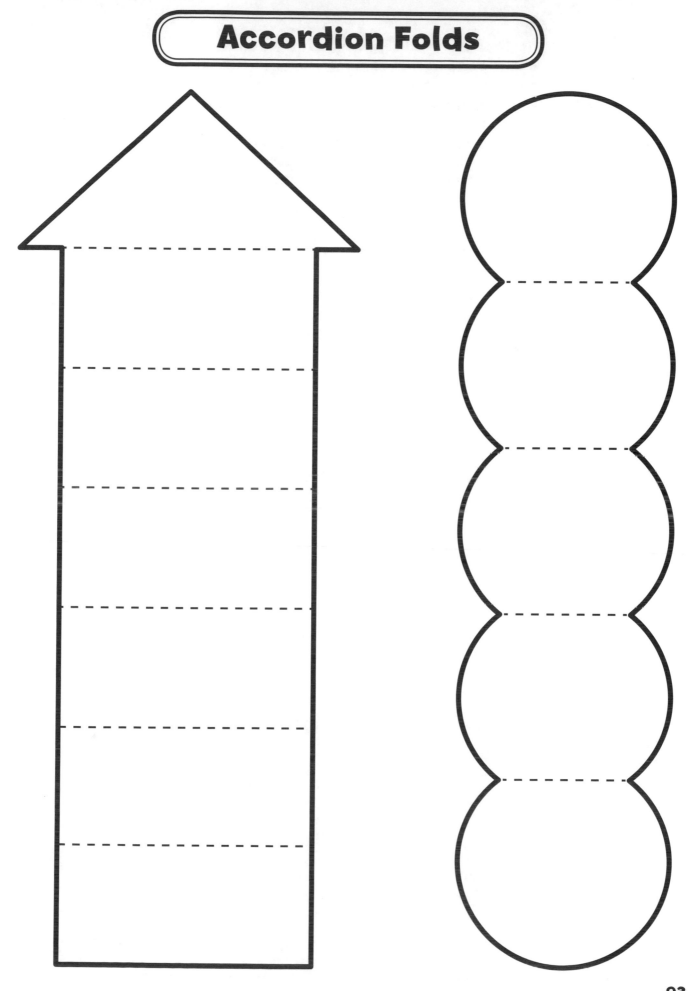

Clamshell Fold

Cut out the clamshell fold on the solid lines. Fold and unfold the piece on the three dashed lines. With the piece oriented so that the folds form an X with a horizontal line through it, pull the left and right sides together at the fold line. Then, keeping the sides touching, bring the top edge down to meet the bottom edge. You should be left with a triangular shape that unfolds into a square. Apply glue to the back of the triangle to attach the clamshell to a notebook page.

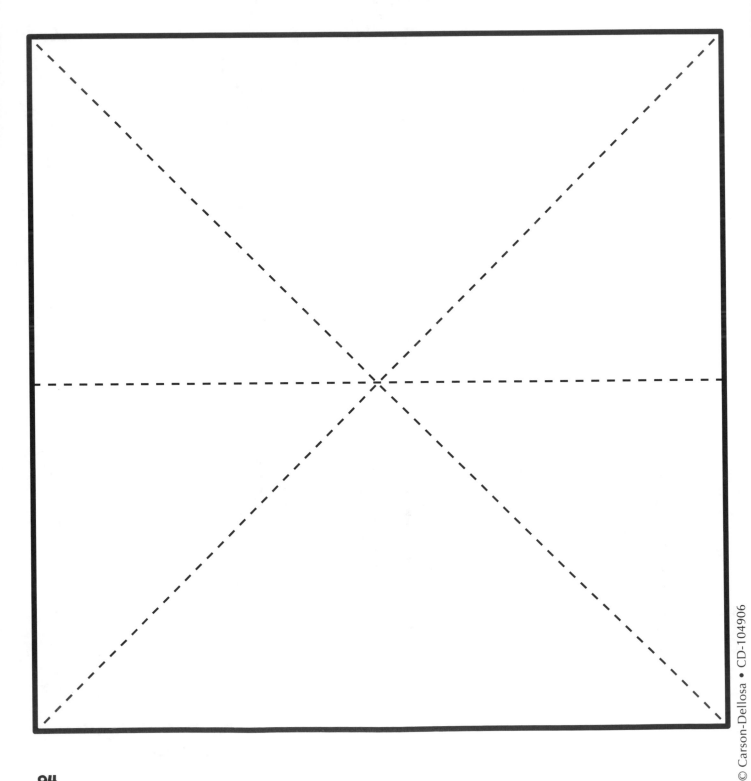

Puzzle Pieces

Cut out each puzzle along the solid lines to create a three- or four-piece puzzle. Apply glue to the back of each puzzle piece to attach it to a notebook page. Alternately, apply glue only to one edge of each piece to create flaps.

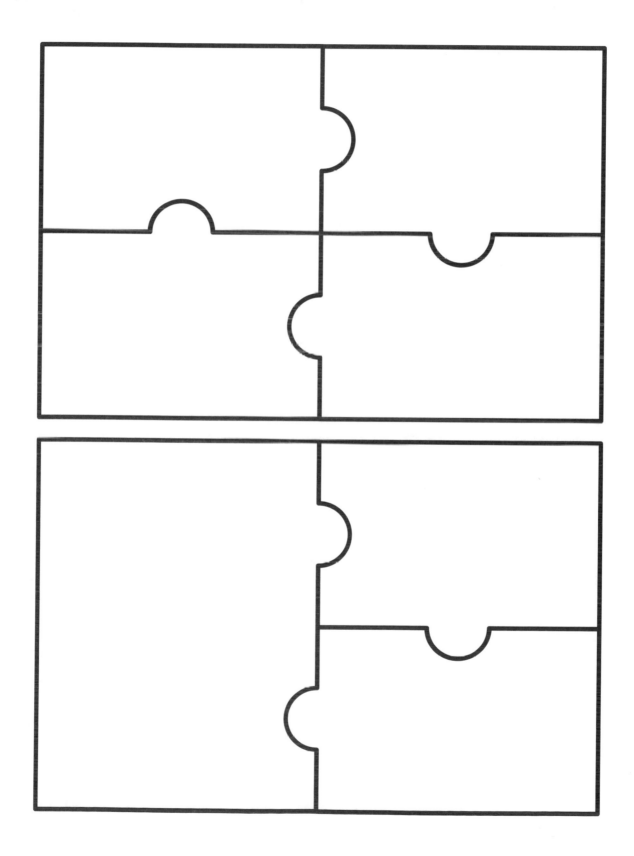

Cut out the two rectangular pieces on the solid lines. Fold each rectangle on the dashed lines. Fold the piece with the gray glue section so that it is inside the fold. Apply glue to the gray glue section and place the other folded rectangle on top so that the folds are nested and create a book with four cascading flaps. Make sure that the inside pages are facing up so that the edges of both pages are visible. Apply glue to the back of the book to attach it to a notebook page.

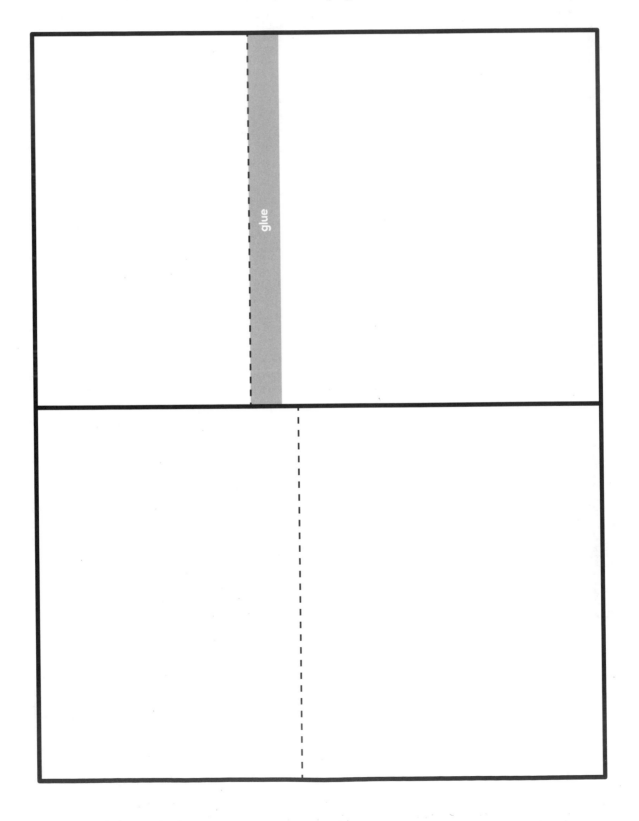